DK EYEWITNESS

T0001230

TOP **10**
PROVENCE
AND THE CÔTE D'AZUR

Top 10 Provence and the Côte d'Azur Highlights

The Top 10 of Everything

CONTENTS

Provence and the Côte d'Azur Area by Area

Streetsmart

Within each Top 10 list in this book, no hierarchy of quality or popularity is implied. All ten are, in the editor's opinion, of roughly equal merit.

Title page, front cover and spine *Blooming lavender flowers at Abbaye Notre-Dame de Sénanque, Provence*
Back cover, clockwise from top left *Bouillabaisse; Arles Old Town; Gorges du Verdon canyon; Abbaye Notre-Dame de Sénanque in lavender field; Street lined with restaurants in Place Rossetti, Nice*

The rapid rate at which the world is changing is constantly keeping the DK Eyewitness team on our toes. While we've worked hard to ensure that this edition of Provence and the Côte d'Azur is accurate and up-to-date, we know that opening hours alter, standards shift, prices fluctuate, places close and new ones pop up in their stead. So, if you notice we've got something wrong or left something out, we want to hear about it. Please get in touch at **travelguides@dk.com**

Welcome to
Provence and the Côte d'Azur

Provence is the most dazzling corner of France. The region's perfect light drew artists such as Renoir and Matisse, while its Riviera glamour has enchanted movie stars and tourists alike. It is a place of history and mystery, fantastic food and unbridled fun. With DK Eyewitness Top 10 Provence and the Côte d'Azur, it's yours to explore.

Thousands of years of migration have left a lasting cultural legacy in Provence, and historic sites such as the Roman amphitheatre in **Nîmes**, the medieval **Abbaye de Sénanque** and the papal vineyards of **Châteauneuf-du-Pape** still operate today. The 20th century shone an even stronger spotlight on the region's timeless villages and towns. Picasso painted Antibes, Van Gogh lost an ear in Arles, and Cézanne captured the Provençal countryside around Aix-en-Provence on canvas.

The Côte d'Azur is the south of France at its most cosmopolitan and lively, from the multinational restaurants of **Marseille** to the glamorous beach clubs of **St-Tropez**. If you grow tired of the high life, it is easy to escape to the perched villages of the **Alpes-Maritimes** and the **Var**, to the wild **Camargue** wetlands or to the **Îles de Lérins** off Cannes. The region is filled with places where you can savour your own off-the-beaten-track paradise.

Whether you're visiting for a weekend or a week, our Top 10 guide brings together the best of everything the region has to offer, from the museums of **Marseille** to the nightlife in **Nice**. The guide gives you tips throughout, from seeking out what's free to avoiding the crowds, as well as ten easy-to-follow itineraries designed to cover a clutch of sights in a short space of time. Add inspiring photography and detailed maps, and you've got the essential pocket-sized travel companion. **Enjoy the book, and enjoy Provence and the Côte d'Azur.**

Clockwise from top: The fishing port of Cassis; carved stonework at Église St-Trophime, Arles; flamingoes in the Carmargue; the Calanque d'En-Vau, Cassis; interior of Notre-Dame de la Garde, Marseille; Les Arénes, Arles; cypress trees at Château de Berne

Exploring Provence and the Côte d'Azur

Provence's most important sights are scattered widely across the region, but a world-class public transport system, with the Nice-Cannes-Aix-Marseille-Avignon TGV train along its spine, connects every hilltop village and coastal town. Here are some ideas to help you make the most of your time.

Two Days in Provence

Day ❶
MORNING

Start your day in **Nice** *(see pp94–9)* with a stroll down **cours Saleya** *(see p20)*. Marvel at the Marche aux Fleurs (flower market), the city's most colourful sight (Tue–Sun), then take a jaunt down the **promenade du Paillon** *(see pp94–5)*.

AFTERNOON

After a lunch of *salade Niçoise* on the seafront promenade des Anglais, relive the French Riviera's glamorous past in the **Villa Masséna** *(see p96)*.

Day ❷
MORNING

Take an early TGV train to explore Avignon's historic **Palais de Papes** *(see pp12–13)*, which overlooks the River Rhône. Have lunch at the venerable **Hiély Lucullus** *(see p131)*.

AFTERNOON

Hire a car and drive through lavender fields to the Roman town of **Vaison-la-Romaine** *(see pp28–9)*. Complete the day with a walk around the bucolic **Abbaye Notre-Dame de Sénanque** *(see pp30–31)*.

Seven Days in Provence

Day ❶
As Day 1 of Two Days in Provence.

Day ❷
Nothing says **Nice** *(see pp94–9)* like Henri Matisse. Take coffee below his former apartment (at what is now Bar L'F, pl Charles Félix), and head up Cimiez hill to marvel at the countless works he bequeathed to the city, now in the **Musée Matisse** *(see p42)*.

Nice's promenade du Paillon offers a leafy stroll in the heart of the busy city.

St-Tropez harbour is lined with fishing boats and super-yachts.

Key

— Two-day itinerary

— Seven-day itinerary

After lunch, ride the coastal train 15 minutes east to bask in the grandeur of the **Prince's Palace** in Monaco (see p103).

Day ❸

Take a boat west along the coast for a lazy day on the sands of **St-Tropez**'s La Fontanette beach. Later, try your hand at *pétanque* on places des Lices, then celebrity-spot around the Vieux Port (see pp24–5).

Day ❹

Head northwest to **Aix-en-Provence** (see 18–19) and follow in the footsteps of Paul Cézanne to the artist's favourite restaurant, the Brasserie Les Deux Garçons on cours Mirabeau. Guided tours are available, via the tourist office, of all the key sights, including the Atelier de Cézanne (his studio, just as he left it) and his family home, the Bastide du Jas de Bouffan.

Day ❺

Start out early. It's a long – if visually stunning – drive northeast to visit the **Gorges du Verdon** (see pp14–15). Stop en route for a bite to eat, and then tour the Corniche Sublime by car. This hair-raising road loops past the Balcons de la Mescla viewpoint, some 700 m (2,300 ft) above the canyon floor. Make sure you save enough time for a hired boat trip out onto **Lac de Ste-Croix** (see p91) before you return to Aix for the night.

Day ❻

Take an early train through the vineyards from Aix to Arles (see pp16–17). Play gladiator in the Roman amphitheatre then picnic amid the ruins. Arles is also the gateway to the breathtaking **Camargue** (see pp26–7). Cycle, kayak or take a boat tour to see flamingoes and other birdlife, white horses and black bulls.

Day ❼

Take a bus to **St-Rémy-de-Provence** (see p83) with its street markets and pavement cafés, which were so loved by local resident Vincent van Gogh. Copies of his paintings are displayed where they were painted, along a picturesque artist's trail. A short bus ride further, **Les Baux-de-Provence** (see p82) has a dramatic ruined castle, two Michelin-starred restaurants and panoramic views over the Provence countryside.

Top 10 Provence and the Côte d'Azur Highlights

Abbaye Notre-Dame de Sénanque, surrounded by lavender fields

TOP 10 Provence and the Côte d'Azur Highlights

Provence's top sights span the region's rich and varied history, from Roman arenas and isolated abbeys to the opulence of the belle époque and the chic resorts beloved of the jet set. Sun-soaked beaches, pretty villages and a mountainous interior have drawn generations of artists, and continue to enchant visitors today.

Palais des Papes ①

This medieval palace, the seat of 14th-century pontiffs, dominates the delightful town of Avignon (see pp12–13).

② Gorges du Verdon

The Verdon river flows through deep limestone gorges into the Lac de Ste-Croix, creating one of Provence's most stunning natural landscapes (see pp14–15).

③ Roman Arles

Arles was one of the Roman Empire's most important cities, and its splendid arena still evokes the age of Caesar (see pp16–17).

④ Aix-en-Provence

Aix is packed with museums and historic buildings. Nearby Mont Sainte-Victoire inspired the Provençal artist Cézanne (see pp18–19).

Map labels:
Bollène · Vaison-la-Romaine · D94 · Orange · D938 · Malaucène · Sault · St Etienne · D1 · Carpentras · Banon · VAUCLUSE · ① Avignon · ⑨ Abbaye Notre-Dame de Sénanque · D900 · Cavaillon · Manosque · Parc Naturel Régional du Luberon · Orgon · ③ Arles · Salon de Provence · Lambesc · Cadarache · The Camargue ⑦ · BOUCHES-DU-RHÔNE · A8 · ④ Aix-en-Provence · A8 · Port St-Louis · A7 · D9 · A51 · D56 · La Couronne · Marseille · Massif de · La Ciotat · Côte des Calanques · Bandol · ⑧ Vaison-la-Romaine

5 Vieux Nice
Nice is a lively and sophisticated city, but its Old Quarter retains its vibrant, historic character *(see pp20–21)*.

6 St-Tropez
Pretty and chic St-Tropez, with its yacht-filled harbour and fantastic beaches, is the place to see and be seen on the Provençal coast *(see pp24–5)*.

7 The Camargue
Vast lagoons inhabited by flamingoes and plains with black bulls are just part of the protected landscape of the regional natural park of the Camargue *(see pp26–7)*.

La Motte · Seyne · Barcelonnette · D900 · 0 km 25 · 0 miles 25 · ALPES-DE-HAUTE-PROVENCE · Sisteron · Parc National du Mercantour · La Javie · Valberg · Tende · Digne-les-Bains · St-André-les-Alpes · ALPES-MARITIMES · Saorge · Les Penitents des Mées · Puget-Théniers · Asse · Gorges du Verdon ② · Castellane · Séranon · Carros · Gréoux-es-Bains · Parc Naturel Régional du Verdon · St-Paul-de-Vence ⑩ · Nice ⑤ · Monaco · Aups · VAR · Salernes · Antibes · Barjols · Le Muy · Cannes · A8 · Brignoles · St-Raphaël · D25 · Massif des Maures · St-Tropez ⑥ · Baume · Cuers · Hyères · Toulon

8 Vaison-la-Romaine
A treasury of archaeological finds has been unearthed in this small town, once one of Provence's most important Roman towns *(see pp28–9)*.

9 Abbaye Notre-Dame de Sénanque
The great Cistercian abbey is a fine example of Romanesque religious architecture *(see pp30–31)*.

10 St-Paul-de-Vence
Walk in the footsteps of artists such as Picasso and Matisse at this former farming community and village that has turned into an artistic hotbed *(see pp32–3)*.

TOP10 ★ Palais des Papes

In 1309, Pope Clement V transferred the papacy to France to escape political turmoil in Rome, and, for 68 years, Avignon became the religious and political centre of Christendom. The magnificent Papal Palace was built in just over 20 years, begun in 1335. Pope Benedict XII was responsible for the sober, Cistercian architecture of the Old Palace; his successor, Clement VI, added the New Palace in Gothic style, creating a massive ensemble of towers and stone walls soaring 50 m (165 ft) above the town centre. It remains a monument to the vast wealth and power of the papacy in the Middle Ages.

3 Consistory Hall

It was in the vast Salle du Consistoire that the pope, cardinals and dignitaries gathered to consider key issues of the day. It is now a museum of artifacts **(left)**, including elegant 14th-century frescoes by Simone Martini.

Palais des Papes

1 Courtyard of Honour

The "meeting" of the two palaces is the best place to compare their respective styles. While the Old Palace resembles a defensive keep, the New Palace has finer stonework. Today the courtyard is the venue for theatrical events taking place during the Avignon Festival (see p70).

2 St John's Chapel

Just off the Consistory Hall, this decorative gem was created by Matteo Giovanetti, a leading Sienese artist. The now-faded frescoes depict the lives of St John the Baptist and St John the Evangelist with exceptional use of perspective across the walls and arched vault.

4 Refectory

It was in the large refectory (tinel) that the pope entertained on feast days, such as a cardinal's appointment or a papal coronation. The pope would eat alone on a dais, while cardinals and guests were arranged around the room according to rank. The spectacular barrel-vaulted wooden ceiling was restored in the 1970s.

5 Stag Room

Clement VI let his extravagant tastes run wild in his study **(below)**. Frescoes of hunting and fishing in a forest setting cover the walls – the most unusual decor in the palace.

6 Benedict XII's Cloister

These four connecting buildings, surrounding a courtyard, date from 1340. Used for staff and guest accommodation, they were decorated by the Italian artist Simone Martini. The Benedictine chapel is also here.

9 Great Chapel

Of massive proportions, 52 m (170 ft) long, 15 m (50 ft) wide and 20 m (65 ft) high, with seven vaulted bays, the Grande Chapelle was the scene of all kinds of religious celebrations, including papal coronations.

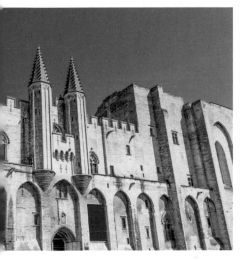

7 Treasury Halls

The papal wealth was stashed beneath the flagstoned floor of the Lower Treasury Hall. The Upper Treasury Hall was effectively the accounts department.

8 Great Audience Hall

This was the meeting place of the popes' forbidding judiciary, against which no appeal was allowed. The vaulted ceiling bears a small section of the Fresco of the Prophet – sadly, much of it was hacked off and sold while the palace was a barracks in the 19th century.

10 Pope's Chamber

The pope's bedroom gives a sense of everyday palace life. The pontiffs slept within blue walls decorated with vine and oak-leaf motifs **(below)**.

NEED TO KNOW

MAP B3

■ Pl du Palais, Avignon
■ 04 32 74 32 74
■ www.palais-des-papes.com

Open daily; Jan–Jun: 10am–5pm; early–mid-Jul: 10am–6pm; mid-Jul–mid-Aug: 10am–7pm; mid-Aug–end Aug: 10am–6pm; Sep–Dec: 10am–5pm.

Adm €12; under-8s free

■ Arrive early in the morning to avoid the crowds – the palace receives up to 4,000 visitors a day in summer.

■ There is a great café on the roof of the palace.

■ The palace's excellent Histopad tablet guides are included with the entry ticket.

■ Ask for the Avignon City Pass when buying your first ticket to an Avignon sight – it includes admission to 10 museums or other attractions within a 24- or 48-hour period.

TOP 10 ⭐ Gorges du Verdon

The aptly named Gorges du Verdon is one of the most spectacular sights in France. Cutting deep into the rock, the Verdon river has created a series of canyons 25 km (15 miles) long and up to 700 m (2,300 ft) deep – a geography that prevented the area being fully explored until 1905. Vividly blue in places, foaming white where it storms through rapids beneath limestone cliffs, the Verdon flows south into the turquoise waters of the Lac de Ste-Croix, formed by damming the river close to Ste-Croix village. For the daring, the canyon offers rock climbing, whitewater rafting and hiking, while the 140-km (85-mile) drive around its magnificent landscapes takes a full day.

1 Route des Crêtes

The Route des Crêtes requires a good head for heights and close attention to the road, but rewards visitors with unbeatable vertiginous views across the most spectacular reaches of the canyon **(above)**.

2 Point Sublime

Close to the village of Rougon, Point Sublime is one of the best places to look down into the rugged landscapes of the gorge. From here, the GR4 trail leads down into the canyon. Sturdy footwear is required, as is a torch (flashlight) to explore the tunnels cut into the cliffs.

3 La Corniche Sublime

The drive along the Corniche Sublime (D71), on the south side of the canyon, genuinely lives up to its name. Stop at the Balcons de la Mescale for a superb view and marvel at Europe's highest bridge, the Pont de l'Artuby, at 125 m (410 ft) high.

4 Moustiers-Sainte-Marie

This lovely village appears to grow out of the surrounding cliffs, with graceful stone bridges connecting houses on either side of the Ravine de Notre-Dame. Noted for its earthenware, it has a small museum and a 12th-century cliffside church, the Chapelle Notre-Dame-de-Beauvoir *(see p48)*.

5 Blanc-Martel Trail

Forming part of the much longer GR4 walking trail through the canyon, the Blanc-Martel Trail **(above)** is the most popular hike through the gorges *(see p57)*, passing cliffs and crossing narrow passes.

Gorges du Verdon

Map locations: Mézel, St-André-les-Alpes, N85, N202, Asse, D953, Moustiers-Ste-Marie, Castellane, Valensole, Gréoux-les-Bains, Riez, La Palud sur Verdon, D952, D11, D71, Quinson, Comps-sur-Artuby, D955, D71, Tavernes, Aups

8 Trigance
This small, attractive village, with its fine views of the rugged mountain peaks that surround it, is a good place to stop for lunch on a motoring tour of the canyon.

9 La Palud sur Verdon
La Palud *(see p122)* is the base for organized walking expeditions into the canyon, whitewater rafting and kayaking on the rapids.

10 Castellane
The pleasant, small town of Castellane *(see p122)* is the largest community in the area and has the widest choice of places to stay and eat. Tour operators here offer a range of activities in the canyon.

6 Lac de Ste-Croix
The hydroelectric dam that created this 10-km (6-mile) long lake **(above)**, south of Moustiers, generates much of Provence's power supply. Electric motorboats, canoes, windsurf boards and catamarans can be hired at Ste-Croix, Les Salles and Bauduen.

7 Aiguines
A stately 17th-century château, with tiled roofs and white turrets **(below)**, overlooks this attractive village. There are panoramic views over the lake.

NEED TO KNOW

Moustiers-Sainte-Marie: **MAP E3**; Office du Tourisme, pl de l'Eglise; 04 92 74 67 84; open daily; Apr–May & Oct: 10am–12:30pm & 2–6pm; Jun & Sep: 9:30am–12:30pm & 2–6pm; Jul–Aug: 9:30am–7pm (9:30am–12:30pm, 2–7pm Sat & Sun); Mar & Nov: 10am–12:30pm &

2–5:30pm; Jan–Feb & Dec: 10am–12:30pm & 2–5pm; www.moustiers.fr

Castellane: **MAP F3**; Office du Tourisme, rue Nationale; 04 92 83 61 14; open Nov–Mar: 10am–noon & 2–5pm Mon, Wed–Fri; Apr & Oct: 9am–noon & 2–6pm Mon–Sat, 9:30am–12:30pm public hols; May–Jun & Sep: 9am–noon & 2–6pm Mon–

Sat, 9:30am–12:30pm Sun & public hols; Jul–Aug: 9am–6:30pm daily; www.verdontourisme.com

■ Hôtel Le Grand Canyon du Verdon (Corniche Sublime/ D71, Aiguines, 04 94 76 91 31) is a good lunch spot.

■ During Apr–Sep, rapid raft trips can be taken down the canyon. Book with an operator in Castellane.

TOP 10 ⭐ Roman Arles

One of the region's most charming towns, Arles was founded by Greek traders but soon gained favour with Caesar and his successors. Its location, on the ancient Via Domitia at the southernmost crossing point of the dangerous river Rhône, saw it grow into one of the most important provincial cities of the Roman Empire. Like many towns of the era, it was built to resemble Rome, with all the amenities. Some of these survive, impressively intact, in the city centre, including the remnants of a Roman theatre, baths and an arena where gladiatorial contests were staged.

Les Arènes ①

One of the most spectacular Roman relics in Provence, this well-preserved arena **(right)** has two floors of arches and seats for 12,000 spectators.

② Porte de la Redoute and Tour des Mourgues

These battered gate towers stand either side of the former Via Aurelia, the highway which ran all the way from Arles to Rome.

③ Église St-Trophime

This spectacular Romanesque church **(left)**, with its beautiful carved stonework, was originally devoted to St Stephen *(see p40)*. In the 10th century it became the church of St Trophimus.

⑥ Théâtre Antique

All that now remains of the Roman theatre, once the hub of Arles, are these two graceful columns **(right)**, also known as the "two widows".

④ Thermes de Constantin

A semi-circular apse marks the site of the once-palatial bathhouse built in the 4th century, in the reign of Emperor Constantine.

⑤ Cryptoportiques du Forum

This amazing labyrinth of chambers beneath the ancient Forum was the city's granary, carved out of the ground during the 1st century BC.

ARLES ARENA

Les Arènes was built to stage the gory gladiator contests so loved by the Romans. Today, from late April until end of September, it hosts plays, concerts, sporting events, and, most famously, bullfights. Most contests are Provençal-style, in which the bull is not harmed, although Spanish-style *corridas* do also take place.

7 Musée Départemental Arles Antique

Highlights of the finest collection of Roman sculpture in Provence include a statue of Venus and a massive Altar of Apollo. There's also a Roman barge that was found on the bed of the Rhône river.

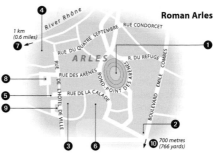

Roman Arles

10 Les Alyscamps

This long avenue of marble sarcophagi marks the site of the Roman necropolis where the city's dignitaries were buried. Among the many legends surrounding the site, it is claimed that Christ appeared here at the burial of St Trophimus, the first bishop of Arles.

8 Place du Forum

Nothing remains today but the name of the Forum, the market which was the very heart of Roman Arles. However the Place du Forum is still the hub of the town.

9 Egyptian Obelisk

Decorated with sculpted lions **(right)**, the square-sided obelisk is likely to have been a trophy from Rome's conquest of Egypt during the reign of Augustus.

NEED TO KNOW

MAP B4

Les Arènes: rond-point des Arènes; open daily; Nov–Feb: 10am–5pm; Mar–Apr & Oct: 9am–6pm; May–Sep: 9am–7pm; closed 1 Jan, 1 May, 1 Nov, 25 Dec; adm €9

Église St-Trophime: pl de la République; open daily; Nov–Feb: 10am–5pm; Mar–Apr & Oct: 9am–6pm; May–Jun: 10:30am–4:30pm; Jul–Sep: 9am–7pm;

adm: cloister €4.50 (under 18s free)

Musée Départemental Arles Antique: av de la 1ère Division Française Libre; open 10am–6pm Wed–Mon; closed 25 Dec; adm €8

Thermes de Constantin: rue du Grand Prieuré; open daily, Nov–Feb: 10am–5pm; Mar–Apr & Oct: 9am–6pm; May–Jun: 10:30am–4:30pm; Jul–Sep: 9am–7pm; closed 1 Jan, 1 Nov, 25 Dec; adm €5

Les Alyscamps: av des Alyscamps; open daily (times are the same as for Thermes de Constantin); adm €4.50

Cryptoportiques du Forum: pl de la Republique; open daily (times are the same as for Thermes de Constantin); adm €4.50

■ Save on entry fees with a Pass Liberté, available for €12. It allows entry to up to five sights and is valid for one month.

TOP 10 ⭐ Aix-en-Provence

Aix-en-Provence is a sophisticated town. Whether in the dignified squares and little streets of the Old Quarter or amid the elegant town houses and tree-lined avenues of the 17th- and 18th-century district, the atmosphere is self-consciously graceful. But it's also lively and fresh: students, studying at one of France's oldest universities, are ubiquitous. The calendar of artistic events is rich, and the markets are the best in the region. The Romans called the town "Aquae Sextiae", after the thermal springs which still flow here.

Cours Mirabeau ①

Created in 1650, Aix's majestic main avenue **(right)** is a tunnel of greenery created by giant plane trees. In their shade stand tall town houses and, on the northern side, smart, lively cafés. A series of fountains adds freshness to the grandeur.

② Rue Gaston-de-Saporta

Running from the town hall to the cathedral is the liveliest thoroughfare of the Old Quarter, buzzing with commerce.

③ Atelier de Cézanne

Cézanne's studio, from 1902 until his death, has been left as it was – a jumble of artist's tools, furniture and still-life subjects **(above)**.

④ Mont Sainte-Victoire

This mountain **(below)** east of Aix, at 1,000 m (3,300 ft) high and 7 km (11 miles) across, exerts an almost mystical power over the region. Cézanne *(see p44)* was so obsessed by its changing moods that he painted it more than 60 times. On its northern slopes is the Château de Vauvenargues, former home and burial place of Picasso *(see p45)*.

EXPLORING AIX

Start at the Office du Tourisme, close to the Rotonde fountain on place du Général-de-Gaulle. Pick up the walking tour leaflet "In the Steps of Cézanne" here. Alternatively, stroll up cours Mirabeau to No. 55 (Cézanne's father's hat shop, now a bank) and enter the Old Quarter through the tiny passage Agard. Return for a drink at the Café des Deux Garçons, No. 53 cours Mirabeau, where Cézanne met with other artists. Chic shops are in Quartier Mazarin, on the other side of the road.

5 Quartier Mazarin

It was here that 17th- and 18th-century Aix nobility built some of their finest town houses. Within this tranquil district of ornamental façades, small galleries and antiques shops, the discreet air of old money remains palpable.

6 Musée Granet

Housed in a former priory, built in 1671, this museum displays European art from the 16th to 19th centuries.

7 Granet XXe

The 16th-century Chapelle des Pénitents Blancs is the airy setting for the collection of Jean Planque, on long-term loan to the Granet. View over 300 works by artists such as Renoir, Monet, Van Gogh and Picasso.

8 Aix Market

The vast and colourful Aix market colonizes all the town's old squares on Tuesday, Thursday and Saturday mornings. From the place de Verdun via the place des Prêcheurs to the place de l'Hôtel de Ville, the streets come alive with stalls selling fresh produce, clothes and antiques.

9 Cathédrale St-Sauveur

This is the focal point of medieval Aix. Notable features are an octagonal, 5th-century baptistry, 12th-century carved cloisters **(left)** and the wonderful Buisson Ardent (Burning Bush) triptych painted in 1476 by Nicolas Froment.

10 Pavillon de Vendôme

Obliged to enter holy orders, local cardinal Louis de Mercoeur built this villa as a love-nest for his mistress in 1665. Its size, decorated façade and extensive gardens, however, suggest a somewhat open secret. It now houses contemporary art exhibitions.

Aix-en-Provence

NEED TO KNOW

MAP D4 ▪ Office du Tourisme: 300 av Giuseppe Verdi; 04 42 16 11 61; www.aixenprovence tourism.com

Cathédrale St-Sauveur: 34 pl des Martyrs de la Résistance; open 8am–6pm daily; adm to cloisters

Musée Granet: pl St-Jean-de-Malte; open Jun–Sep: 10am–7pm Tue–Sun,

Oct–May: noon–6pm Tue–Sun; closed 1 Jan, 1 May, 25 Dec; adm €6

Atelier de Cézanne: av Paul Cézanne; open Oct–Mar: 9:30am–12:30pm & 2–5pm Tue–Sat (to 6pm Apr–Jun & Sep, 9:30am–6pm Jul & Aug); closed 1–3 Jan, 1 May, 25 Dec; adm €6.50; www.cezanne-en-provence.com

Pavillon de Vendôme: 32 rue Célony; open

10am–12:30pm & 1:30–5pm Wed–Mon (to 6pm mid-Apr–mid-Oct); closed Jan; adm €3.70

Granet XXe: pl Jean-Boyer; open as Musée Granet; adm €5.50

▪ Aix is traditionally associated with *calissons* – yellow candied sweets made with ground almonds and fruit, and topped with a layer of icing.

TOP 10 ★ Vieux Nice

Foreign aristocrats and the rich and famous may have colonized other parts of the city, but Vieux Nice belongs firmly to the Niçois, who claim it with Mediterranean gusto. Tiny streets throb with arm-waving commerce, and Baroque architecture slots into a warren of hanging washing, galleries, craft workshops and food stalls. The noise, mouth-watering aromas and vivid colours recall the city's long links with Italy – Nice became French in 1860. The lively atmosphere lasts well into the night in the many trendy bars, restaurants and clubs here.

1 Cathédrale Ste-Réparate

When the Dukes of Savoy ruled Nice they worshipped in this soaring, 17th-century church. It boasts a majestic polychrome cupola **(below)** and, within, the extravagance of the stuccoed Baroque decor is breathtaking.

2 Rue St-François-de-Paule

This busy thoroughfare is home to two of the city's best-loved institutions: Maison Auer, a wonderful *chocolaterie*, at No. 7, and Alziari, the olive and *"grand cru"* olive oil specialists, at No. 14.

3 Cours Saleya

The great square (or rather, oblong) **(right)** bursts into life every Tuesday to Sunday morning with the world-famous flower market. Come evening, bar and restaurant terraces buzz. On Monday mornings the flower market is replaced by an antiques and flea market. This is Vieux Nice's focal point, colourful and vigorous.

4 Palais Lascaris

Nice's most sumptuous 17th-century Baroque palace is now home to an exceptional museum of historic musical instruments.

5 Colline du Château

The castle that was once here was destroyed in 1706, but the hill still boasts splendid views. A botanical park covers the slope below.

6 Place St-François

This delightful square, overseen by an 18th-century clock tower and a Baroque palace, is the site of the fish and herb market, held around the dolphin fountain (open Tuesday to Sunday).

7 Chapelle de la Miséricorde

If you see only one of Nice's Baroque churches, make sure it is this one. The splendour of the decoration **(below)** makes it one of the world's best examples of the style.

8 Opéra de Nice

This ornate building is home to ballet, classical music and opera. The theatre, designed by François Aune, a pupil of Gustave Eiffel, was reconstructed in 1885 following a fire which entirely destroyed the original. It was classified a *monument historique* in 1993.

9 Rue Pairolière

In this charming narrow street **(right)**, food shops spill over with *socca* (pancakes), salt cod and spicy meats, jostling for space amid Provençal fabrics and jewellery. Stroll through the crowds, soaking up the exciting mix of aromas, colours and Niçois accents.

BAROQUE CHURCHES

Vieux Nice is celebrated for its Baroque churches. In addition to those mentioned here, there are several others worth visiting: Ste-Rita (rue de la Poissonnerie); Gesù (rue Droite); St-Martin-St-Augustin (pl St-Augustin); St-François-de-Paule (rue St-François-de-Paule); St-Suaire (rue St-Suaire) and the Chapelle des Pénitents Rouges (rue Jules Gilly – Latin Mass every Sunday morning).

NEED TO KNOW

MAP H4 ■ Office du Tourisme: 5 prom des Anglais; 04 92 14 46 14; en.nicetourisme.com

Palais Lascaris: 15 rue Droite; open 10am–6pm Wed–Mon

Chapelle de la Miséricorde: cours Saleya; open 2:30–5:30pm Tue

Cathédrale Ste-Réparate: pl Rossetti; open 9am–noon & 2–6pm Tue–Fri; 9am–noon & 2–7:30pm Sat; 9am–1pm & 3–6pm Sun (closed during Mass)

Opéra de Nice: 4–6 rue Saint-François de Paule; 04 92 17 40 79

■ Save energy: take the free lift up Colline du Château from Quai des Etats-Unis.

■ Vieux Nice is for pedestrians only; there's parking on pl Masséna.

10 Quartier du Malonat

Daily life courses through the tiny streets and squares, and beneath the washing and *trompe l'oeil* house decorations in the most authentic sector of Vieux Nice.

Vieux Nice

450 metres
(490 yards)

Following pages Boats moored at Nice harbour

TOP 10 ⭐ St-Tropez

Within the space of a short stroll it is easy to see why this sun-soaked, congenial fishing village, with its pretty harbour, red-tiled houses and fabulous sandy beaches, seduced the painters, writers and free spirits that made it famous. Despite all its hype as a world-famous tourism mecca of the rich and famous, "St-Trop" retains a good deal of its original charm – brightly painted fishing boats still moor in the Port de Pêche, although today they are increasingly outnumbered by gleaming yachts.

ARTISTIC MECCA

How did St-Tropez transform itself from undiscovered fishing village to holiday hotspot? Painter Paul Signac *(see p41)* must take half the blame: he arrived on his yacht in 1887, fell in love with the light and colour and decided to stay. Other painters followed, along with writers and would-be artists, attracted by warm weather and easy living. The film industry discovered the St-Trop scene in the 1950s, with the jet set following in its wake. Brigitte Bardot became its ultimate symbol in the Swinging Sixties and the place has never looked back.

1 Notre-Dame-de-l'Assomption

This ebullient Italian Baroque church, built in the early 1800s, contains a gilded bust of the town's patron saint, Tropez (or Torpès). According to legend, the Roman legionary converted to Christianity and was martyred by Emperor Nero. His body was pushed out to sea by the Romans before washing up where the town now stands.

2 Vieux Port

The quayside of the Old Port, quai Jean Jaurès **(above)**, is lined with leisure vessels year-round. In summer the waterside buzzes with artists, and pedestrians hoping to spot a celeb.

3 Citadel

The 17th-century ramparts surround a fort built to protect the village from Barbary corsairs. The citadel also has the Musée d'Histoire Maritime.

St-Tropez and the church of Notre-Dame-de-l'Assomption

NEED TO KNOW

MAP F5 ▪ Office du Tourisme: quai Jean Jaurès; 04 94 97 45 21

Open Oct–Apr: 9:30am–1pm & 2–5:30pm Mon–Sat; May–Sep: 9:30am–6pm Mon–Sat, 10am–5pm Sun; www.sainttropez tourisme.com

Notre-Dame-de-l'Assomption: rue Commandant Guichard; open 9:30am–noon daily

Musée de l'Annonciade: Pl Georges Grammont; open Jan–Mar & Nov–Dec: 10am–5pm Tue–Sun; Apr–Jun & Oct: 10am–6pm Tue–Sun; Jul–Sep: 10am–7pm daily (mid-Jul–Sep: to 9pm Mon); adm €6

▪ Le Café on place des Lices, earlier the Café des Arts, is where St-Tropez's artists hung out in the 1950s and 1960s heyday.

▪ Visit the place des Lices on Tuesday or Saturday morning, when the square is filled with antiques, flowers and fruit stalls.

④ La Fontanette

The small La Fontanette beach, just east of La Ponche, is not as stunning as those further afield, but is the only one within walking distance of the town. It is ideal for a swim while you are exploring St-Tropez.

⑤ Place des Lices

This market square, immortalized by the painter Charles Camoin *(see p44)*, still has some of the atmosphere that he captured in his work. Crowded with open-air café tables, and shaded by plane trees, it is the perfect place in which to watch locals playing *pétanque* (boules).

⑥ Tour Suffren

Built in AD 880 by Guillaume I, Duke of Provence, this round tower overlooking the harbour was once part of a larger castle, the Château Suffren. The tower overlooks the fishing harbour where old boats are moored.

⑦ Musée de l'Annonciade

Close to the Vieux Port, a pretty 16th-century chapel has been wonderfully converted to house a world-class collection of paintings by famous artists connected with St-Tropez, including Bonnard, Derain, Dufy, Matisse, Rouault and Signac *(see p42)*.

⑧ Plages de Tahiti and Pampelonne

St-Tropez's beaches begin 4 km (2.5 miles) southeast of the town, on a long bay, the Anse de Pampelonne *(see p54)*. The 9-km (5-mile) sweep of sand is divided into smaller stretches, each with its own name.

⑨ Sentier des Douaniers

The "Customs Officers' Path" is part of a longer coastal path with spectacular views of the Côte d'Azur. The many tiny pebbly or sandy bays offer bathing opportunities away from the crowds. Energetic walkers can follow the path for 35 km (21 miles) to Cavalaire.

⑩ La Ponche

La Ponche **(above)** is the core of the original fishing village. With narrow streets, painted shutters and ochre walls, it looks much as it did before tourism arrived.

🔟⭐ The Camargue

Black bulls, white horses and pink flamingoes: these are the classic images of the Camargue delta where the Rhône meets the sea and France's only cowboys gallop across the flattest land in France. It's a 1,000 sq km (386 sq miles) zone of lagoons, salt flats and marshes; remote, romantic and rich in birdlife. Large stretches are protected and inaccessible, but open to all are the beautiful nature views and stunning sunsets.

1 Abbaye de St-Gilles

This once-vast medieval abbey, in St-Gilles-du-Gard, was severely damaged in 1562. The carved façade **(below)**, one of Provence's most beautiful, has survived intact.

2 The Salt Pans

The largest salt pans in Europe **(below)**, in the southeast of the Camargue region, cover 100 sq km (40 sq miles) and produce 800,000 tonnes of salt a year. Reach the great mounds of salt via a little train at Salin d'Aigues Mortes.

3 Domaine de la Palissade

Visitors can explore the rich flora and fauna of this natural reserve either on foot (walks range from 30 minutes to 3 hours 30 minutes in duration) or, from April to October, in the saddle on a Camargue horse.

4 Musée de la Camargue

A converted sheep barn in Mas du Pont de Rousty is a fine setting for a little museum dealing with the interaction of man and nature in the Camargue, from the 19th century to today.

5 Les-Saintes-Maries-de-la-Mer

The tiny main street of this old village teem with crowds in summer, but its seaside charm remains intact. The May pilgrimage of the Romani people marks the legendary arrival of Mary Magdalene, Mary Jacoby, Mary Salome and their servant Sara, who is patron saint of Romani peoples.

6 Domaine de Méjanes

The banks of Vaccarès lagoon are a good place to spy Camargue white horses and flamingoes.

CAMARGUE BIRDLIFE

The Camargue is a paradise for birdwatchers, particularly in spring when migrant birds visit on their journey north. The iconic flamingoes stalk the delta's shallow lagoons, but there are other birds as well. This is the only French breeding site of the slender-billed gull; the red-crested pochard also breeds here.

⑦ Parc Ornithologique du Pont-de-Gau

Next to the information centre is this splendid bird park **(below)**. Aviaries dotted around two acres of marshland house unusual birds that are very difficult to spot in the wild.

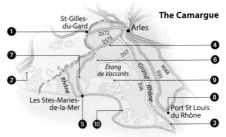

The Camargue

⑨ Parc Naturel Régional de Camargue

The HQ of the Camargue National Nature Reserve of the Vaccarès lagoon and surrounding area is in La Capelière, and has displays on ecosystems and climate. Nature trails and observation posts let you test out your new knowledge.

⑩ Plage de Beauduc

The "beach at the end of the world" **(below)** is the spot for wild camping and wild watersports in summer. Vehicles are not permitted here.

⑧ Port St Louis du Rhône

This port town has an 18th-century tower, which once served as a look-out post. The tower now houses an ornithological museum and offers superb views of the salt marshes.

NEED TO KNOW

MAP A4 ■ Parc Ornithologique: Pont-de-Gau; www.parc ornithologique.com

Open daily (except 25 Dec) Adm €7.50

Musée de la Camargue: Mas du Pont de Rousty; open Mon–Fri (Feb–Oct: daily); closed 1 Jan, 1 May, 25 Dec, adm €7; www. museedelacamargue.com

Salin d'Aigues Mortes: 04 66 73 40 24; open Apr–Nov; adm €11 (museum and train)

Parc Naturel Régional de Camargue: La Capelière; 04 90 97 00 97; open Apr–Sep: daily, Oct–Mar: Wed–Mon; adm €4

Port St Louis du Rhône (Office du Tourisme): Tour Saint Louis–Quai Bonnardel; 04 42 86 01 21; open

times vary, check website for details; www.portsaintlouis-tourisme.fr

Domaine de la Palissade: Salin de Giraud; open Mar–Oct: daily, Nov & Feb: Wed–Sun; adm €3, riding tours from €20; www.palissade.fr

■ For the real Camargue experience be sure to visit a *manade* (farm).

TOP 10 ⭐ Vaison-la-Romaine

Vaison is a delightful town, boasting a magnificent array of Roman relics, including a graceful single-arched bridge that miraculously survived the devastating floods of the Ouvèze river in 1992. Founded by the Celtic Vocontii tribe, the town was named Vasio Vocontiorum after the Roman conquest, and for four centuries it flourished until the collapse of the empire, when the original site was abandoned for the safer precincts of the walled Ville Haute and its castle on the opposite bank of the Ouvèze. Between 1907 and 1955, a local abbot, Chanoine Sautel, excavated the Roman city.

1 Puymin

Named for the hill on which it stands, this district **(left)** was the most important part of the town in Roman times, containing the *praetorium* (court house), a theatre, temples and shops. There are also several well-preserved houses that can be explored. A broad road runs from the theatre to the main gate.

2 Maison des Messii

The House of the Messii must once have been home to one of the town's most important families. Columns and the foundations of an atrium, baths, a temple to household gods, a dining room and living rooms can all still be seen.

3 House with the Silver Bust

Named after a statue found here and now on show in the museum, the ruins of this once grand, mosaic-floored villa are enhanced by copies of statues found here and elsewhere on the site.

4 House with the Dolphin

The House with the Dolphin was named after the marble statue of Cupid riding a dolphin found here, now in the museum. The villa once had a façade supported by 18 columns.

5 Musée Théo Desplans

A muscular, life-size marble nude of the Emperor Hadrian **(left)**, a statue of his empress Sabina, a gorgeous silver bust found at the Villasse site, and a six-seater public latrine are among the more interesting archaeological finds in this excellent small museum.

6 Portico of Pompey

This impressive portico, built by the family of Caesar's great rival Pompey, is a huge, 65-m (210-ft) array of columns, which originally surrounded an inner garden. Built around AD 20, it was demolished during the 5th century. Copies of statues that originally stood on the site now grace the niches – the originals are preserved in the nearby museum.

⑦ Théâtre Antique

The 1st-century AD theatre **(below)** is a dazzling display of Roman building skill, with 34 semi-circular rows of stone benches, seating up to 7,000 spectators, rising to a columned portico.

⑧ Nymphaeum

The Nymphaeum was a rectangular sacred pool with a fountain, which was covered by a roof supported by four columns. Traces of the building still remain, as does the sacred spring which provided the water supply. It now forms an elegant backdrop to an open-air theatre.

⑨ Haute Ville and the Pont Romain

Vaison's 2,000-year-old Roman bridge connects the upper town on the south bank with the north bank of the Ouvèze. The prettily restored old quarter **(below)**, with its 17th-century town houses, courtyards and fountains, is ringed by ramparts and entered through a massive, 14th-century stone gateway.

⑩ Château

At the highest point of the old town stands a dramatic, part-ruined castle **(above)**, built in 1160 by the Count of Toulouse. Three main wings and a formidable keep tower surround an inner courtyard.

TOP 10 ⭐ Abbaye Notre-Dame de Sénanque

Surrounded by the lavender fields of the Luberon, this lovely abbey exudes tranquillity, but its past was anything but peaceful. Founded in 1148, Sénanque's golden age was the 13th century, but in 1544 it was torched by heretic Vaudois, in 1580 it was stricken by the plague, and by the 17th century only two monks were left. The French Revolution and the anti-monastic laws of the 19th century were equally harsh but, since the 1970s, the abbey's fortunes have been restored, and a small community of monks is now in residence here.

1 Apse
The three windows of the raised, semi-circular apse symbolize the Holy Trinity.

2 Nave and Transept
The barrel-vaulted nave **(below)** and aisles of Sénanque are five bays long, and three stone steps lead from the nave to the square crossing, with its eight-sided dome.

4 Abbey Shop
The Cistercians believe in work as well as prayer, and the fruits of their labours are here. This shop sells their own lavender essential oil and honey from their hives, and books and products made in other convents and monasteries across France.

5 Channels
The Cistercians came to this plateau seeking isolation, and built their abbey next to the region's only river, the Senancole. They channelled the water to flow through and under the abbey, providing sanitation and irrigation for the gardens.

3 Cloister
The dove-grey limestone columns of the cloister **(right)**, decorated with delicate carvings of leaves, flowers and vines, are superb works of craftsmanship, dating back from 1180 to 1220.

7 Dormitory

The dormitory is a huge, vaulted space, paved with flagstones. Arched windows **(left)** at regular intervals along its walls and two large, circular windows at each end make this otherwise austere room feel pleasantly light and airy.

8 Tomb of the Seigneur de Venasque

In one corner of the east arm of the transept is the only non-Cistercian element of the church – a Gothic tomb marks the burial place of Geoffroy, the 13th-century Lord of Venasque and at one time the abbey's benefactor.

9 Lavender Fields

The abbey of Notre-Dame de Sénanque is surrounded by fields of lavender **(left)**, which make a spectacular setting for the buildings in the summer.

ST BERNARD AND THE CISTERCIANS

With their complete lack of decoration or comfort, Provence's most outstanding Romanesque monasteries, Sénanque, Silvacane (see p82) and Le Thoronet (see p88), reflect the austere ideals of the Cistercian order, founded in 1098 by St Bernard, abbot of Clairvaux in north-east France. Rejecting the ostentation and luxury of the powerful Benedictine order, St Bernard advocated a rigorous and pure monastic life within simple, yet graceful and harmonious buildings.

NEED TO KNOW

MAP C3 ▪ 04 90 72 18 24 ▪ www.senanque.fr ▪ Spiritual retreats: email frere.hotelier@ndsenan que.org

Open non-guided visits: 10–11am & 1–5pm Mon–Sat, 1–5pm Sun; guided tours (In French, plus HistoPad tablet available in 10 languages): book online at least 48 hours ahead; arrive 10 mins before tour. Mass: 8:30am Mon, 11:45am Tue–Sat, 10am Sun & bank hols. Closed mid-Nov–Jan (am), Ascension (sixth Sun after Easter), 15 Aug, 1 Nov, during snow.

Adm: €8.50 (tours)

▪ The most striking approach to Sénanque is from Gordes, with a panorama of the abbey as the road descends into the craggy valley in which Sénanque stands.

6 Calefactory

The calefactory and scriptorium reflects St Bernard's injunctions against luxury: with two fireplaces, this was the only heated room in the monastery, which enabled monks to read without their hands freezing.

10 Chapterhouse

The walls of the square chapterhouse, are lined with stone seats **(above)**. Here the monks sat each day to hear the abbot read a chapter from the Rule of St Benedict or a sermon from the Bible.

TOP 10 ⭐ St-Paul-de-Vence

Set in alpine hinterland with panoramic views of the Riviera coast, the medieval village of St-Paul-de-Vence (one of the oldest in the region) sits in a breathtaking location. It has been a magnet for artists and art lovers since the 1920s; Picasso, Dufy, Matisse and Chagall were among the artists who regularly visited to unleash their creativity. The village's maze of medieval streets, full of modern and contemporary art galleries and workshops, is a delight to stroll through.

1 Fondation Maeght

Home to one of Europe's largest collections of 20th-century art, Fondation Maeght was set up by Cannes art dealers Aimé and Marguerite Maeght. Their private art collection formed the basis of the foundation.

2 Place de la Grande Fontaine

Built in 1615, the pretty fountain **(above)** in Place de la Grande Fontaine is of typical Provençal design. It is one of the village's most photo-graphed sights. The square hosted a weekly market in the Middle Ages and has long been a favourite subject with artists.

3 Rue Grande

Running between the Porte de Vence and Porte de Nice, the rue Grande is St-Paul's main thoroughfare. It is lined with the studios and workshops of local artists and artisans. The street resembles an open-air art museum where you can admire the work of cutting-edge talents in the windows of upscale commercial galleries.

4 Les Remparts

Visitors can walk around the village's well-preserved 16th-century ramparts – originally built to resist assault from Savoy and Piedmont – and enjoy a panoramic view of the vineyards and olive groves that cloak the surrounding beautiful hilly countryside.

5 Chapelle St Charles-St Claude

Perched on a promontory above the village's ramparts, this chapel was founded in the 17th century. In the early 2010s Nice artist Paul Conte decorated it with colourful murals depicting scenes from the lives of the saints to whom the church is dedicated.

St-Paul-de-Vence village

6 Place de Gaulle

Locals meet at this square, also known as Place du Jeu de Boules, for a friendly game of pétanque under the plane trees. Tournaments take place throughout the summer.

7 Donjon (Tour de la Mairie)

The dungeon was one of the first structures built in the village and its base formed part of the original château. The bell tower was added in the 1440s. The building now houses the town hall.

8 Cimetière

Marc Chagall, who lived in St-Paul-de-Vence for almost 20 years, is the most famous resident of the village's cemetery **(left)**. His modest, cedar-shaded grave is a place of pilgrimage for admirers, who leave small stones in a growing pile as a visible tribute.

ARTISTS IN ST-PAUL-DE-VENCE

Attracted by the colours, light and sweeping views, the first artists to visit St-Paul-de-Vence in the 1920s were Paul Signac, Raoul Dufy and Chaïm Soutine. They were soon followed by other greats, including Matisse, Chagall and Picasso and the village became a major cultural hub. Poet and screen writer Jacques Prévert lived in a small house (La Miette) in the village for 15 years and the American writer James Baldwin made the village his home between 1970 and 1987.

9 La Chapelle Folon (Chapelle des Pénitents Blancs)

Artist Jean-Michel Folon worked with local artisans to decorate this 17th-century chapel with stained-glass windows, sculptures, murals and mosaics. The chapel is immaculately preserved as a celebration of him.

10 Église Collégiale

First built in the 14th century and completed in the 18th century, this small church **(below)** has as its highlight the 1680 Chapelle Saint Clément, decorated in ornate Baroque style.

NEED TO KNOW

MAP G4 ■ Office du Tourisme: 2 rue Grande; 04 93 32 86 95; open 10am–6pm Mon–Fri, 10am–1pm & 2–6pm Sat; closed public hols

■ *Fondation Maeght:* 623 chemin des Gardettes; 04 93 32 81 63; open 10am–6pm daily (Jul–Aug: to 7pm); adm €16 adults; €11 children aged 10–18; free for children under 10

■ *La Chapelle Folon (Chapelle des Pénitents Blancs):* Pl de l'Église; 04 93 32 86 95; open May–Sep: 10am–12:30pm & 2–6pm daily, Oct–April: 10:30am–12:30pm & 2–4pm daily; closed Nov, 25 Dec, 1 Jan; adm €3, free for children under 12

■ *Église Collegiale:* Place de l'Église; open 8:15am–4:15pm Mon–Fri, 10am–6pm Sat, Sun & public hols

■ Eat at La Colombe d'Or (www.la-colombe-dor.com) on pl du Général de Gaulle (closed end Oct–25 Dec), a 1920s inn adorned with paintings by artists.

The Top 10
of Everything

Magnificent 15th-century frescoes in Notre-Dame des Fontaines, La Brigue

🔟 Moments in History

Carvings in the Vallée des Merveilles

1 Early Settlers
Rock carvings found in the Grotte d'Observatoire in Monaco and paintings in the Grotte Cosquer near Marseille date from 350,000 BC. Between 2500 and 2000 BC, dwellers in the Vallée des Merveilles (see p114) left behind over 10,000 carvings of beasts and figures.

2 Foundation of Aix
In 123 BC, Greeks from Phocaea (modern Turkey), who had settled in Marseille since 600 BC, asked Rome for help against the invading Celtic tribes. After defeating the Celts, the Romans founded the town of Aquae Sextiae (Aix-en-Provence) (see pp18–19).

Roman mosaic found in Aix-en-Provence

3 Advent of Christianity
In AD 40 St Honorat brought Christianity to Provence, founding the first monastery on Île de Lérins. Camarguais legend, however, claims that Christianity was introduced to Provence by Mary Magdalene herself (see p39).

4 Franks and Saracens
With the fall of the Roman Empire in AD 476 Provence was pillaged by barbarians, eventually coming under the rule of the Franks. From the 8th century Provence was raided and attacked by the Saracens for about 200 years. They were finally defeated in 973 by Guillaume le Libérateur, Count of Arles.

5 Dawn of a Dynasty
In 1297 François Grimaldi, a supporter of the papacy in the Guelph-Ghibelline feuds which beset 13th-century Italy, seized Monaco and its castle to found the dynasty that still rules there today.

6 The Avignon Papacy
Pope Clement V relocated to Avignon in 1309 to escape strife-torn Rome, the first of a succession of nine French pontiffs who were to reside in the Provençal town. In 1348 Clement VI bought the city and Avignon remained the seat of the papacy until 1377 (see pp12–13).

Pope Clement V at Avignon

King René, ruler of Provence

7 Union with France

In 1486 King René of Naples, the last of the Anjou dynasty who ruled Provence from 1246, died without issue, and most of the region became part of France. Nice and the Alpes Maritimes, however, remained part of the Kingdom of Savoy, before finally passing to France in 1860.

8 Plague and War

In the second half of the 16th century religious strife erupted in the Luberon between reforming Vaudois and Huguenot factions and conservative Catholics. The plague of 1580 added to the region's woes.

9 La Marseillaise

When the French Revolution erupted in July 1789, the citizens of Marseille were among its staunchest supporters, marching to a tune that became known as "La Marseillaise", now France's national anthem.

10 Resistance and Liberation

After the Nazi invasion of 1940, Provence was ruled by the collaborationist Vichy government, until it was occupied by Germany and Italy in 1942. Guerrilla fighters in the *maquis* (scrubland) resisted the Occupation. On 15 August 1944, Allied troops landed, liberating Provence after two weeks of fighting.

TOP 10 FIGURES IN HISTORY

1 Julius Caesar
Caesar besieged Marseille after its citizens sided with his biggest political rival Pompey in 49 BC.

2 François Grimaldi
Grimaldi disguised his troops as monks to seize control of Monaco in 1297.

3 Catherine Ségurane
Known as Catarina Segurana in Niçois, this brave washerwoman helped lead Nice's defence against the Franco-Ottoman invasion in 1543 *(see p46)*.

4 Petrarch
The renowned Italian Renaissance poet (1304–74), who spent much of his early life in Avignon, was a critic of the ostentatious French papacy.

5 Nostradamus
Born in St-Rémy-de-Provence, the scholar (1503–66) published his book of prophecies in 1555.

6 Napoleon Bonaparte
Bonaparte landed at Golfe-Juan on 1 March 1815 to regain his empire, only to be defeated at Waterloo.

7 Louis-Auguste Blanqui
Born in Puget-Théniers in 1805, the socialist was one of the leaders of the revolutionary Paris Commune of 1871.

8 Jacques Cousteau
Toulon-based naval officer Cousteau perfected the aqualung in the 1940s, pioneering the sport of scuba diving.

9 Antoine de St-Exupéry
The aircraft of the French author and pilot vanished in 1944 while on a reconnaissance flight over Provence.

10 Simone Veil
Born in Nice, Veil (1927–2017) served as Health Minister of France in the 1970s and advanced women's legal rights.

Simone Veil

TOP10 Roman Sights

Théâtre Antique d'Orange

1 Théâtre Antique d'Orange

One of the best-preserved theatres from the Roman empire (see p125), built during the reign of Augustus (c.27–25 BC), is the highlight of the Parc de la Colline St-Eutrope. A triumphal arch decorated with relief carvings commemorates Julius Caesar's victories over Gaul.

2 Temple of Apollo, Riez
MAP E3

The four Corinthian columns of the 1st-century-AD temple to Apollo, standing tall and alone among fields just outside Riez on the Valensole plateau, are all that remain of the once-prosperous Roman settlement of Reia Apollinaris. Eight ancient pillars, perhaps scavenged from another Roman building, are now in the early Christian church nearby, which dates from the 4th or 5th century BC and is one of the oldest surviving churches in France.

3 La Trophée d'Auguste, La Turbie

This majestic Roman monument (see p112), built from local white stone, was erected in 6 BC to mark the boundary between Italy and Gaul and to honour Augustus's Gallic conquests. Towering over the small village of La Turbie, high above Monte Carlo, with breathtaking views over the Riviera, it still has the power to impress.

4 Les Arènes de Fréjus
MAP F4 ■ Rue H Vadon
■ Open Apr–Sep: 9:30am–12:30pm & 2–6pm Tue–Sun; Oct–Mar: 9:30am–noon & 2–4:30pm Tue–Sat
■ Closed public hols ■ Adm

Like other large Roman arenas in Provence, the amphitheatre at Fréjus (see p87), which can seat up to 10,000 people, is still used regularly for bull-fights and classical music concerts. It was originally built in the 1st and 2nd centuries AD. Nearby are parts of the original Roman wall.

Glanum, near St-Rémy

5 Les Antiques de Glanum

Twin temples, a Roman forum, baths and a fortified gate can be seen at Glanum, near St-Rémy (see p83), which also has traces of a 4th-century Greek settlement. A triumphal arch (10 BC) marks Gallic victories.

6 Pont du Gard
MAP A3

The Romans considered this 49-m- (160-ft-) high three-tiered bridge to be clear testimony to their empire's greatness. The top tier was part of an aqueduct that supplied Nîmes with water for up to 500 years. Constructed in the 1st century AD from dressed stone blocks without mortar, the bridge is an incredible 275 m (900 ft) long and represents an astonishing feat of engineering.

7 Arc de Triomphe, Cavaillon
MAP C3

This twin-arched triumphal gate, lavishly adorned with carved vines and dramatic Corinthian columns, was built during the reign of the Emperor Augustus, in the 1st century AD. There are other interesting Roman finds in the town's archaeological museum.

8 Arles

Remnants of Provence's most important Roman settlement (see pp16–17) can still be seen in numerous spots around this lovely town.

9 Pont Flavien, St-Chamas

One of the best-preserved Roman bridges in France, Pont Flavien (see p84) was built in a single arch over the River Touloubre in the 1st century AD, as part of Emperor Augustus's Via Julia Augusta, which linked Piacenzia (Palantia) in Italy to Arles. Many Roman bridges had triumphal arches at either end, but this is the only one with arches that have survived intact.

10 Vaison-la-Romaine

Another Roman gem, discovered in 1907 (see pp28–9).

Magnificent Pont du Gard, spanning the Gardon river

🔟 Places of Worship

Frescoed interior of Notre-Dame des Fontaines

① Notre-Dame des Fontaines, La Brigue

MAP H2 ■ Rue Notre-Dame des Fontaines ■ Open mid-Apr–Sep: 10am–12:30pm & 2–5:30pm ■ Closed Thu ■ Adm

This chapel, 4 km (2.5 miles) from La Brigue, is covered with remarkable frescoes by Giovanni Canavesio and Giovanni Baleison, dating from 1492.

② Chapelle des Pénitents Blancs, Les-Baux-de-Provence

MAP B4 ■ Open 10am–5pm daily (Apr–Sep: to 7pm)

Frescoes in this simple chapel, painted in 1974 by local artist Yves Brayer, depict a typical Provençal nativity scene with shepherds. More of Brayer's work can be seen in the nearby museum (see p82).

③ Notre-Dame-du-Puy, Grasse

MAP G4 ■ 8 pl du Petit Puy ■ Open Oct–Mar: 9am–noon & 2–5pm Mon–Sat; Apr–Sep: 9am–noon & 2–5pm Mon, 10am–noon & 1–6pm Tue–Sat

Fragonard's *Christ Washing the Disciples' Feet* is the main reason for visiting this 13th-century church. It also contains three magnificent religious works by Rubens, all painted in 1601: *The Crown of Thorns*, *The Crucifixion of Christ* and *The Deposition of St Helena*.

④ Église St-Trophime, Arles

This is one of the most attractive of all Provençal churches. It's also one of the oldest – a church stood here as early as AD 450. In the 11th century the church (see p16) was rebuilt and dedicated to St Trophime.

Carvings on the Église St-Trophime

⑤ Notre-Dame-de-Nazareth, Vaison-la-Romaine

MAP C2 ■ Rue Alphonse Daudet ■ Open Jun–Sep: 9am–6pm daily; other times call 04 90 36 05 65

This evocative 6th-century cathedral has a superb arcaded apse and 12th-century cloister.

6 Église des Saintes-Maries-de-la-Mer

The bell tower of this fortified church is a Camargue landmark. The church has lent its name to the capital of the region, and its sturdy walls offered refuge from raiders. The most colourful sight within is a carved boat with statues of the Virgin and Mary Magdalene and a statue of St Sara in the crypt. The Romani pilgrimage in May (see p26) marks the legendary arrival of Mary Magdalene by boat.

7 Cathédrale, Fréjus

Constructed in the pink stone typical of Fréjus, the 13th-century cathedral (see p87) has a beautiful Renaissance doorway. Its interior is dominated by superb pointed arches, and the cloister ceiling, with its scenes of the Apocalypse, is unique.

8 Notre-Dame-de-l'Assomption, Puget-Théniers

MAP G3 ■ Open 8am–6pm daily
Built by the Knights Templar, the 13th-century parish church of this mountain village has a lovely triptych altarpiece, Notre-Dame-de-Bon-Secours, which depicts the Passion, painted by Antoine Ronzen in 1525. The group of wooden sculptures have been attributed to the sculptor Matthieu d'Anvers or Flemish or Burgundian craftspeople.

9 Abbaye de Montmajour

The extraordinary abbey of Montmajour (see p82) was built on a rocky island amid the Rhône marshes. It was an important pilgrimage site and became wealthy from selling pardons for sins. The cloister is decorated with mythical and biblical scenes.

The stunning Abbaye de Montmajour

10 Chapelle du Rosaire de Vence

MAP G4 ■ Open 10am–noon, 2–5pm Tue, Thu, Fri (Mar–Oct: to 6pm); 2–5pm Wed, Sat (Mar–Oct: to 6pm); Mass 10am Sun, followed by guided tour ■ Closed 1st two weeks Dec, public hols ■ Adm
The dazzling white interior walls of this little chapel are adorned with black line drawings of the Stations of the Cross. They are unmistakably the work of Henri Matisse (see p45), who designed this building in 1949.

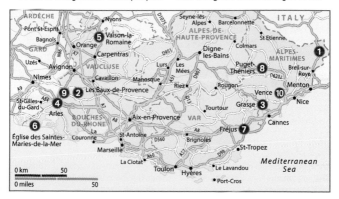

🔟 Art Galleries

Exterior of the Musée National Marc Chagall, Nice

1 Musée National Marc Chagall, Nice

One of the jewels of Provence, this museum *(see p97)* houses the world's largest collection of works by Marc Chagall, including 17 canvases from his Biblical Message series.

2 Musée Fernand Léger, Biot

Mosaics in primary colours, carried out to Léger's own design, identify this strikingly modern museum. The Cubist painter planned to build a studio here just before his death in 1955, and the museum on the site *(see p113)* exhibits more than 400 of his works.

3 Musée de l'Annonciade, St-Tropez

This serene former chapel *(see p25)* houses a riveting art collection. Opened in 1955, it boasts works by Pierre Bonnard, Raoul Dufy, Paul Signac and Charles Camoin, whose *St-Tropez, la place des Lices et le Café des Arts* (1925) is one of the most famous images of the town.

4 Fondation Maeght, St-Paul-de-Vence

This small museum *(see p33)* has a world-class array of modern art, including paintings by Léger, Bonnard and Chagall, sculpture by Miró and a mosaic pool by Braque.

5 Musée Bonnard, Le Cannet

MAP G4 ▪ 16 bd Sadi Carnot ▪ Open 10am–6pm Tue–Sun (Jul & Aug: to 8pm daily) ▪ Adm

Pierre Bonnard spent most of 1926–47 in Le Cannet, and this museum, in a belle époque villa, displays some of his finest canvases. Links with the Musée d'Orsay in Paris bring frequent special exhibitions.

6 Musée d'Art Moderne et d'Art Contemporain (MAMAC), Nice

A dazzling work of contemporary architecture in its own right, with marble-faced towers and glass corridors, the contemporary art museum *(see p95)* contains works by some of the 20th century's greatest avant-garde artists.

7 Musée Matisse, Nice

Founded in 1963, nine years after the painter's death, the Musée Matisse *(see p95)* is located in the 17th-century Villa des Arènes. There are sketches, paintings and bronze sculpture by Matisse, as well as some of his personal effects.

The façade of the Musée Matisse, Nice

Les Musées Jean Cocteau, Menton

8 Les Musées Jean Cocteau, Menton

MAP H3 ■ Le Bastion: open 10am–12:30pm & 2–6pm Wed–Mon; Collection Séverin Wunderman: closed for renovation until further notice ■ Adm ■ www.museecocteaumenton.fr

Jean Cocteau (1889–1963), a famous poet, playwright, author and film director, converted a 17th-century fort (Le Bastion) into his personal museum. The nearby Collection Séverin Wunderman houses 1,800 pieces donated by the eponymous art enthusiast and Cocteau devotee in a futuristic building.

Renoir's studio, Cagnes-sur-Mer

9 Musée Renoir, Cagnes-sur-Mer

Auguste Renoir's house (see p105) at Les Collettes, where the painter came in hope that the climate would cure his rheumatism, houses 11 of his paintings. The house is surrounded by beautiful olive groves.

10 Musée Picasso, Antibes

Housed in the Château Grimaldi, used as a studio by Picasso in 1946, the museum (see p104) contains more than 50 of his paintings, sketches, prints and ceramics, as well as works by Léger and Miró.

TOP 10 MASTERPIECES OF PROVENCE

1 Wagons de Chemin de Fer à Arles
Painted in 1888 by Van Gogh, this work set in Musée Angladon (see p128) is only one of his many canvases on permanent display in this region.

2 La Joie de Vivre
This 1946 work in the Musée Picasso Antibes (see p104) is one of Picasso's most important from his time here.

3 La Partie de Campagne
Fernand Léger's painting is on display at the Fondation Maeght (see p115).

4 Nu Bleu IV
This 1952 work in the Musée Matisse (see p95) is among the best known of Matisse's blue paper cut-outs.

5 Coronation of the Virgin
Enguerrand Quarton's 1453 altarpiece painting can be seen in the town's Musée Pierre de Luxembourg.

6 Venus Victrix
One of Renoir's most magnificent bronzes (1914) stands amid the olive groves at Les Collettes.

7 Les Baigneuses
Prior to his monumental versions of The Bathers, Cézanne painted this smaller scene around 1895. It is on display at the Musée Granet (see p19).

8 The Burning Bush
Nicolas Froment's 1476 triptych in the Cathédrale de St-Saveur (see p19) was commissioned by Provence's king, René.

9 La Terrasse à l'Estaque
This early Cubist work (1908) in the Musée Cantini (see p77) is part of a trio Raoul Dufy painted of the village.

10 L'Orage
Pointillist Paul Signac's 1895 work in St-Tropez's Musée de l'Annonciade (see p25) depicts St-Tropez harbour.

L'Orage by Paul Signac

🔟 Painters in Provence

Van Gogh's *The Red Vineyard Near Arles* (1888)

1 Vincent van Gogh
The Dutch Post-Impressionist created hundreds of his most vivid, powerful landscapes and self-portraits during his few years in Arles and St-Rémy. The sunshine of Provence is said to have changed the way Van Gogh (1853–90) saw light and colour.

2 Yves Klein
Born in Iceland, Klein (1928–62) became one of the leading lights of the Nice School of New Realists, who aimed to create art from everyday materials. His *Anthropométries*, in Nice's Musée d'Art Moderne et d'Art Contemporain (see p95), was created by three nude women, covered in his signature blue paint, rolling over a huge white canvas.

3 Marc Chagall
The Russian-born painter (1887–1985) moved to St-Paul-de-Vence in 1949. His light-filled work was often inspired by biblical themes. Canvases from his Biblical Message series of paintings are in the Musée National Marc Chagall (see p97) in Nice.

4 Fernand Léger
Léger (1881–1955) is known for his strong Cubist paintings and his love of bold lines and pure primary colours. He devoted the later years of his life to working in ceramics in Biot (see p113), and eventually bought a villa in the village.

5 Paul Cézanne
Born in Aix, where he lived most of his life, Cézanne (1839–1906) painted hundreds of oil and water-colour scenes of his home town and the nearby Mont Sainte-Victoire (see pp18–19) in his Post-Impressionist style. He captured the soul of Provence better than any painter.

Cezanne's *François Zola Dam* (1877–8)

6 Raoul Dufy

Dufy (1877–1953) embodies the values of the Fauvist school, with its revolutionary use of bright, intense colour. He found Nice the perfect background for his vivid work.

7 Henri Matisse

Matisse (1869–1954) lived in Nice from 1917 until his death. His earlier works were inspired by the vivid light and colours of the Riviera. During World War II he retreated to Vence, where he designed the unique Chapelle du Rosaire (see p41), and its wonderful Stations of the Cross, vestments and furnishings.

8 Paul Signac

A master of the Pointillist style, Signac (1863–1935) came to St-Tropez in 1892. He found, in the sparkle of sun on sea, the perfect subject for Pointillism's technique of using a myriad of tiny rainbow dots to depict swathes or blocks of colour.

Signac's _Antibes, the Pink Cloud_ (1916)

9 Pablo Picasso

Picasso (1881–1973) was influenced by the sights and colours of Provence, where he lived in exile from his native Spain for much of his life. He learned to make ceramics from the potters of Vallauris (see p108) and helped revive the craft.

10 Paul Guigou

This realist painter (1834–71) illustrated the landscapes of his native Vaucluse. Among his best-known works is _Deux Lavandières devant la Sainte-Victoire_, in the Musée Grobet-Labadié in Marseille (see p76).

TOP 10 WRITERS IN PROVENCE

Albert Camus

1 Albert Camus
This French author and existentialist (1913–60) wrote his respected autobiography at Lourmarin.

2 Alexandre Dumas
Dumas (1802–70) used the Château d'If (see p77) as the grim backdrop to _The Count of Monte Cristo_ (1845).

3 Jean Giono
Born in Manosque, this son of Provence (1895–1970) wrote lyrically about the region's people and landscapes.

4 Frédéric Mistral
This Nobel Prize-winner (1830–1914) wrote epic poems based on local lore.

5 Alphonse Daudet
Daudet (1849–97) is best remembered for _Tartarin de Tarascon_, the popular tale of a Provençal bumpkin.

6 Graham Greene
The English novelist (1914–91) retired to Nice, where he wrote _J'Accuse – the Dark Side of Nice_ (1982).

7 F Scott Fitzgerald
The US writer (1896–1940) stayed at Juan-les-Pins in 1926 while he wrote his novel _Tender is the Night_.

8 Edith Wharton
Wharton (1862–1937) spent winters at her villa in Hyères, where she finished _The Age of Innocence_, the first book by a woman to win the Pulitzer Prize.

9 Marcel Pagnol
The famous French author and film director (1895–1974) wrote _L'Eau des Collines_ (1963), later filmed as _Jean de Florette_ and _Manon des Sources_.

10 Colette
Colette (1873–1954) wrote charmingly of St-Tropez in _La Naissance du Jour_ ("break of day"), published in 1928.

🔟 Provençal Legends

Red rocky outcrop in Roussillon

1 Roussillon
The red cliffs of Roussillon (see p129) are not coloured by accident. In medieval times the local lord's wife, Sirmonde, fell in love with a troubadour. The lord had him killed and Sirmonde threw herself off a cliff, staining the rocks with her blood.

2 Man in the Iron Mask
Who was the Man in the Iron Mask? Louis XIV's troublesome brother? A meddling royal priest? No one knows. Certainly, he was dangerous enough to be clamped in a mask and locked away on Île Ste-Marguerite (see p70) from 1687. You may visit the island fort and see his cell.

3 Pont d'Avignon
In 1177 a shepherd boy named Bénézet received orders from God that a bridge should be built across the Rhône. Avignon people were

The famous Pont d'Avignon

sceptical, so the lad picked up a rock that 30 strong men couldn't shift and carried it to where Pont St-Bénézet (see p128) was to begin.

4 Avignon's Hidden Treasure
Pope John XXII was rumoured to be an alchemist, who used magic to win his election. He had an amulet to detect poison (supposedly because other churchmen kept trying to kill him) and made enough gold to fill an underground room. When Benedict XIII, the last Avignon anti-pope (see p13), was forced to flee, he walled the room up. The room, with its treasure, has never been found.

5 St Maximin-la-Ste-Baume
After reputedly landing in Provence, Mary Magdalene spread the Christian word, before spending her last years praying in a cave in the Ste-Baume mountains. Her remains were discovered in the 13th century and may be seen in a reliquary in the Gothic basilica (see p88).

6 Catherine Ségurane, Nice
Washerwoman Cathérine led Niçois resistance against the Turkish fleet that besieged the city in 1543. She knocked out the Turkish standard-bearer with her washboard, before lifting her skirts and putting the rest of the Turks to flight. The battle was eventually lost, but Cathérine has a statue in Vieux Nice (see pp20–21).

7 Les Pénitents des Mées

In AD 800 a group of monks ogled female Saracen prisoners being led to the Durance river and were turned to stone as punishment *(see p122)*. There they remain – a 2-km (1-mile) line of rocks, some 100 m (300 ft) high, looking like repentant monks with their cowls up.

Les Pénitents des Mées

8 Saintes-Maries-de-la-Mer

After being set adrift in a boat from Palestine, Mary Jacoby (sister of the Virgin Mary), Mary Magdalene, Mary Salome, Lazarus and a servant girl, Sara, landed on the Provençal coast. They were the first Christians in Gaul. The "relics" of Jacoby and Salome are found in the town's church *(see p84)*, as are those of Sara, patron saint of the Romani people.

9 Lost "City of God"

The Latin inscription on a rock near St-Geniez indicates the site of a 5th-century "Theopolis", or City of God. No other trace has ever been found. However, pheno-mena here, including strange lights and odd weather, add to the mystery.

10 La Tarasque, Tarascon

The Tarasque, a dragon-like beast, terrorized Tarascon *(see p81)* in the 1st century AD, until St Martha sprinkled it with holy water. The Tarasque remains central to the town's lively June festival.

Provençal nativity scene

🔟 Provence Villages

1 Moustiers-Ste-Marie

At the entrance to the Verdon gorges *(see pp14–15)*, Moustiers hangs like a pendant from the rock face soaring above *(see p14)*. The glorious tangle of vaulted streets and tiny squares are divided by rushing streams. High above, tucked against the rocks, is the Notre-Dame-de-Beauvoir chapel *(see p119)*. The village is also celebrated for its pottery.

2 Les-Baux-de-Provence

Emerging dramatically from its crag on the edge of the Alpilles hills, Les-Baux *(see p82)* was home to one of the finest courts in medieval Provence. Abandoned for centuries, the ruined castle and labyrinthine streets now throb with summer tourists. But the site remains majestic, the atmosphere lively and the views over mountains and plains quite breathtaking.

3 Sisteron

At the northern gateway to Provence, Sisteron's minuscule vaulted streets and unexpected stair-cases climb the vast sentinel rock overlooking the Durance river. It's a harsh setting for a village with a tumultuous past. Up top, the 14th-century citadel *(see p120)* was all but impregnable and now affords unbea-table views over the rugged landscape.

Sisteron, overlooking the Durance

Cobbled street in Séguret

have sculpted the red-and-gold earth into cliffs, canyons and weird formations. Villagers have applied the local red, yellow and brown ochre to their houses, to enchanting effect.

8 **Roquebrune-Cap-Martin**
A winning partnership of the sort only found on the Côte d'Azur. Beneath Roquebrune are the grandiose belle époque villas of the super-rich on the Cap-Martin peninsula. Up above are the winding streets, vaulted passageways and 10th-century château *(see p104)* of the original village.

4 **Séguret**
Encircling its hillside like a belt, Séguret *(see p129)* stares out from the edges of the Dentelles de Montmirail mountains across the nearby wine plain. It's an almost impossibly pretty spot of tiny, pedestrianized streets, medieval edifices and contemporary artists and artisans.

9 **Cassis**
Cassis is overseen by France's highest coastal cliffs, whose scale reinforces the intimacy of the narrow little harbour and old town centre down below. Tourists crowd the beaches – the best bathing is in the creeks to the west – but Cassis remains a fishing port *(see p82)*, and retains its authenticity.

5 **St-Paul-de-Vence**
St-Paul-de-Vence *(see pp32–3)* was a farming community living quietly within its medieval environs and 16th-century walls until the 1920s. Then it was discovered by the Côte d'Azur artistic community (Picasso, Matisse, Léger) and has been fashionable ever since, with good reason. Both artists and tourists find the tiny streets, ramparts and church remains utterly charming.

The fishing port at Cassis

6 **Bormes-les-Mimosas**
This delightful village *(see p88)* seems to tumble down the hillside, with a jumble of steep alleyways, hidden corners and stone houses overcome with flowers the village's name is very appropriate. Walk up to the top of the hill and enjoy the splendid views of the Mediterranean from the ruined medieval castle.

10 **Fontaine-de-Vaucluse**
The *"fontaine"* is actually Europe's most powerful natural spring – it pumps out 2.5 million cubic m (55 million gallons) of water a day, and is the source of the River Sorgue. It's a spectacular setting for a lovely village *(see p126)*, made even more romantic by its association with the Italian poet, Petrarch, who lived here in the 14th century.

7 **Roussillon**
Roussillon *(see p129)* is perched magnificently above an extraordinary landscape. The mining of ochre and subsequent erosion

TOP 10 Areas of Natural Beauty

Lac d'Allos, Parc National du Mercantour

1 Parc National du Mercantour
MAP G2

Mercantour National Park *(see p114)*, sprawling over 700 sq km (270 sq miles), is one of Europe's largest, and its rocky slopes are home to rare species including chamois, ibex, moufflon and marmot. Golden eagles and the rare lammergeier vulture soar above the peaks.

2 Gorges du Cians and Gorges du Daluis

High in the mountains of Haute-Provence and the Alpes-Maritimes, the parallel canyons of the Gorges du Cians *(see p113)* and the Gorges du Daluis are awesome ravines, carved by icy, fast-flowing streams running down from wine-red cliffs. The main landmark is the Gardienne des Gorges, a huge boulder shaped like a woman's head, standing at the north end of the Gorges du Daluis.

3 Parc Naturel Régional du Luberon

The Luberon region contains a wide range of habitats *(see p125)*. The northern mountains are wild and exposed, while the central massif shelters the southern slopes, creating a gentler environment. Moorland, cedar forest, chalk hills and deep river gorges shelter wild boar, eagles, owls and beavers.

4 Parc National de Port-Cros
MAP F6

Port-Cros is the smallest of the Îles d'Hyères, and the national park protects the delightful island and 18 sq km (7 sq miles) of sea around it from the development that has overtaken so much of the coast. On land, it shelters beautiful butterflies and rare sea birds, while the clear waters offer excellent scuba diving *(see p91)* and snorkelling.

5 Mont Ventoux

The dramatic peak of Mont Ventoux *(see p125)*, at 1,910 m (6,260 ft), seems to guard the gateway to the region. Bare of trees, its higher slopes are known as the *désert de pierre* (stone desert) and are snow-covered from December to April. It has featured in the Tour de France, and even the strongest cyclists dread the treacherous ascent.

The peak of Mont Ventoux

6 Les Alpilles
MAP B4

The chalky hills of the "Little Alps" rise no higher than 500 m (1,640 ft) but display an arid beauty. This miniature sierra stretches for 24 km (15 miles) between the rivers Rhône and Durance, and the GR6 hiking trail which crosses it is one of the finest walks in Provence.

7 The Camargue
A landscape of lagoons, marshes, wild bulls and France's only cowboys (see pp26–7).

8 Réserve Géologique de Haute-Provence
MAP E2

If dinosaurs and fossils are your thing, this park in the limestone country around Digne is the place to head for. It is the largest of its kind in Europe, covering 1,900 sq km (730 sq miles) of rock, rich in fossils from ancient seas and tropical forests dating back 300 million years.

9 Massif des Maures
Thickly wooded with forests of cork and holm oak, pine, myrtle and sweet chestnut, the dramatic Massif des Maures (see p89) is wild, hilly and sparsely inhabited, even though it is only a stone's throw from the busy coastal hotspots. It is home to France's only surviving wild tortoises, and makes a welcome change from crowded beaches.

10 Gorges du Loup
The clifftop village of Gourdon, set in rugged limestone country, stands above the dramatic Gorges du Loup (see p115), the most accessible of the gorges and canyons that slash through this craggy landscape. The Loup stream plunges over high cascades and has carved deep potholes such as the Saut du Loup ("Wolf's Leap").

Waterfall in the Gorges du Loup

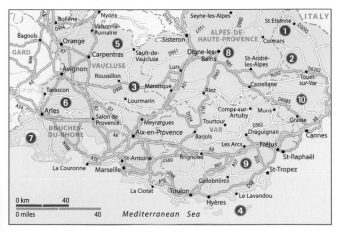

🔟 Beaches in Provence

Dramatic Calanque d'En-Vau

1 Calanque d'En-Vau, Cassis

Calanques (see p76) are inlets formed where the chalk cliffs plunge to the sea; many are found between Cassis and Marseille. En-Vau is the prettiest and one of the more accessible – a 90-minute walk from the nearest Cassis car park. At the foot of the white, pine-clad rocks, the setting of sand and luminous sea is intimate, wild and unforgettable.

2 Plage Notre Dame, Île de Porquerolles
MAP E6

No cars are allowed on the island, so it's a walk or cycle-ride along the rocky, 3-km (2-mile) track from the port to the loveliest beach in France *(see p91)*. Pine-fringed, it boasts white sand, clear, calm waters, no commerce and few people – your private slice of paradise.

3 Plage de Pampelonne, St-Tropez
MAP F5

Everyone has his or her "place" on St-Trop's largest beach *(see p25)*. Famous beach clubs cater to everyone, from the super-rich to nudists to families. The 5-km (3-mile) sandy stretch across the headland from the town also has extensive public areas. There's space in which to escape the crowds and appreciate natural beauty.

4 Plage de la Garoupe, Cap d'Antibes

Between them, Antibes and Juan-les-Pins have 25 km (16 miles) of coast and 48 beaches, slotted into rocky creeks or opening out into sandy expanses. The prettiest is La Garoupe *(see p110)*, on an inlet of the peninsula. It's highly fashionable and very crowded in summer – but with very good reason.

5 Plage d'Agay, St-Raphaël

As the red rocks of the Esterel hills tumble into the clear blue sea, they give the coastline around St-Raphaël an untamed allure. The small creeks are enticing; equally alluring, but bigger,

Esterel coastline around Plage d'Agay

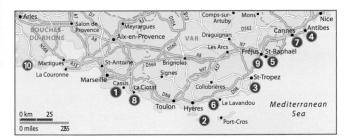

sandier and more accessible, is the Bay of Agay *(see p106)* – perfect for families.

6 Plage de l'Eléphant, Le Lavandou
MAP F5

Le Lavandou has 12 beaches covering the full seaside spectrum, from the great sandy stretch of the Grande Plage to the nudist creek of Rossignol. L'Eléphant is the most appealing. The approach is only by sea or over rocks, a feature which usually ensures relative tranquillity.

Sunbathers enjoy Plage de l'Eléphant

7 St-Honorat, Îles de Lérins

A short ferry ride leads from the crowds of Cannes to this island owned by Cistercian monks *(see p57)*. The presence of the monastery seems to discourage the more brazen holiday-makers so the pretty rock outcrops and tiny beaches here remain calm and, unusually for Provence, positively underpopulated.

Calanque de Figuerolles

8 Calanque de Figuerolles, La Ciotat
MAP D5

Steps on the eastern edge of town lead to this extraordinary creek. On either side are cliffs, while further back are terraces of fig trees and pines. Out front, the blue sea laps around weird rock formations. It is a world unto itself.

9 Plage de St-Aygulf, Fréjus
MAP F5

Long, wide, sandy and safe, the main beach at St-Aygulf, near Fréjus *(see p87)*, has the additional advantage of being in a Nature Preservation Area. This protects the Étangs de Villepey – great, wild, freshwater lagoons on the other side of the road, where 217 different bird species have been noted.

10 Piémanson Beach, The Camargue
MAP B5

This is a beach beyond civilization. You must thread your way between salt flats and lagoons before arriving at the flat, exposed sands of France's last truly "wild beach".

🔟 Gardens of Provence

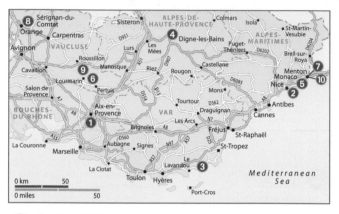

① Jardins d'Albertas, Bouc-Bel-Air

MAP D4 ▪ DN 8 ▪ 04 42 22 94 71 ▪ Open May, Jun, Sep: 2–6pm weekends and public hols; Jul–Aug: 3–7pm daily ▪ Adm ▪ www.jardins albertas.com

Laid out in the 1750s, these terraced gardens remain a majestic mix of French and Italian influences – ordered in the geometrical style of France, but with the fountains and statuary favoured by Italy.

Jardin de la Villa Ephrussi de Rothschild

② Jardin de la Villa Ephrussi de Rothschild, St-Jean-Cap-Ferrat

Baroness Rothschild's mansion is legendary (see p103), and its gardens are of similar sumptuousness. Eight themed areas (Spanish, Florentine, Japanese and more) are rich with plants, sculptures and fountains, and the views are exquisite.

③ Domaine du Rayol, Le Rayol-Canadel

MAP F5 ▪ Av Jacques Chirac ▪ Open 9:30am–6:30pm daily (Nov–Mar: to 5:30pm; Jul–Aug: to 7:30pm); for guided tours timings visit www.domainedurayol.org ▪ Adm (includes guided tour)

On one of the most magnificent sites on the coast, Domaine du Rayol offers an overview of Mediterranean-style plant life. Gathered around a pergola, a fine mosaic of eight gardens recreates landscapes of areas of the world with Mediterranean climates.

④ Jardin Botanique des Cordeliers, Digne-les-Bains

MAP E2 ▪ Pl des Cordeliers ▪ Open mid-Mar–mid-Nov: 9am–noon & 2–6pm Mon–Fri (to 7pm Jul–Aug) ▪ Closed Wed pm ▪ Guided tours in English by appt: 04 92 30 81 50

Named after a 13th-century convent previously on the site, this garden features more than 650 species of aromatic plants from the region and abroad. Beds are arranged in squares, according to a classical design.

Cacti in the Jardin Exotique

5 Jardin Exotique, Monaco

Crisscrossed by winding paths, this garden *(see p107)* features a large collection of cactuses, succulents and other semi-desert plants – 6,000 varieties in all. A prehistoric cave and anthropology museum are also within the garden grounds.

6 Château Val Joanis, Pertuis

MAP D4 ■ D973 ■ 04 90 79 20 77 ■ Open 10am–1pm & 3–7pm Mon–Sat ■ Adm

These award-winning gardens were planted in 1978 on three sheltered terraces, mimicking the 17th-century French style. They include a classic *potager* (vegetable garden) and an orchard amid roses and cypresses.

7 Jardin Botanique Val Rahmeh, Menton

MAP H3 ■ Av St Jacques ■ Open 9:30am–12:30pm & 2–5pm Wed–Mon (Apr–Sep: 9:30am–12:30pm & 2–6pm) ■ Closed 1 May, 25 Dec ■ Adm

More than 700 tropical plants crowd these terraces, established in 1905 by Lord Radcliff, a former governor of Malta. Val Rahmeh specializes in spices, wild-flowers, medicinal plants, succulents and rare varieties of tomato and potato.

8 Harmas Jean-Henri Fabré, Sérignan-du-Comtat

MAP B2 ■ Rte d'Orange ■ 04 90 30 57 62 ■ Opening times vary, check website ■ Adm ■ www.harmasjean henrifabre.fr

This fascinating walled garden was planted by etymologist Jean-Henri Fabre to observe the lives of insects, which he recorded in exquisite watercolours in his books.

9 Jardin de la Louve, Bonnieux

MAP C3 ■ Chemin St Gervais ■ Opening times vary, check website ■ Closed early Oct–mid-Apr ■ Adm ■ www.lalouve.eu

It's worth the special effort to visit this private, ultra-contemporary topiary garden, created by Hermès stylist Nicole de Vésian to harmonize with the surrounding landscape.

10 Serre de la Madone, Menton

MAP H3 ■ 74 rte de Gorbio ■ 04 93 57 73 90 ■ Open 10am–6pm Tue–Sun (Jan–Mar: to 5pm); guided tours 3pm daily ■ Closed Nov, Dec, 1 Jan ■ Adm ■ www.menton.fr/Jardin-Serre-de-la-Madone

Anglo-American Lawrence Johnston was a leader among expats who left their mark on Riviera gardens in the early 20th century. His hillside spread is so well landscaped, it barely seems structured. Terraces harbour enclosed spaces dedicated to themes or exotic plants, and there are fountains, water gardens and a collection of statues.

Water garden in Serre de la Madone

Sporting Activities

Skier in the Alpes-Maritimes

1 Skiing
Skiing is concentrated where Provence and the Alps meet *(see p114)*. In the Ubaye valley, Pra-Loup, Le Sauze and Super-Sauze offer international-standard facilities as, in the Allos valley, do La Foux and Seignus. Meanwhile, there's family-friendly skiing on Mont Ventoux – notably at Mont Serein.

2 Climbing
For some of France's finest, toughest rock climbing, head for the Buoux cliffs in the Luberon *(see p125)*, the Gorges du Verdon, with their 933 routes *(see pp14–15)* or the creeks and Calanques between Marseille and Cassis *(see pp76–7)*. Easier conditions can be found in the Dentelles de Montmirail *(see p126)*.

Climbing in the Gorges du Verdon

3 Sailing
Almost all the coastal resorts have well-equipped pleasure ports and cater for both the beginner and the experienced. The island of Porquerolles and Bandol village on the mainland have renowned sailing schools.

4 Canoeing
The classic river trip is to canoe down the Gorges du Verdon – a two-day, turbulent, 24-km (15-mile) trip from Carajuan Bridge to Lac de Ste-Croix *(see p15)*. Less adventurous canoeists might prefer paddling the gentler Sorgue, from Fontaine-de-Vaucluse *(see p126)*.

Canoeing on the Verdon river

5 Mountain Biking
The marked trails, up and down mountains, through vineyards, forests, gorges and creeks, are endlessly inviting. Figanières is a key centre in the Upper Var, while the Alpes-de-Haute-Provence region has some 1,500 km (900 miles) of marked tracks.

6 Golf
The finest golfing can be found at the Frégate golf course, St Cyr, where the sea views are sensational *(see p91)*. Other courses offering good golf in lovely surroundings include Bluegreen Esterel at St-Raphaël, the Ballesteros-designed Pont Royal at Mallemort and Golf de Châteaublanc outside Avignon.

Scuba Diving

The richness of marine life, clear waters and a sprinkling of wrecks all draw divers to the Mediterannean coast. The Îles d'Hyères are noted for their seascapes and for the underwater "discovery trail" on Port-Cros *(see p70)*. Cavalaire and Marseille remain, however, the best-equipped centres.

Windsurfing

The breezy Var and Bouches-du-Rhône coasts are ideal for water-sports fans. As the Mistral whistles across the Camargue, so windsurfers take advantage at Saintes-Maries-de-la-Mer and Port-St-Louis *(see p27)*.

Walking

From the coastal paths to mountain tracks inland, Provence could have been created for walkers. Strollers may amble around bays or along woodland paths, while serious hikers can take to the National Hiking Trails (Grandes Randonnées or GR) which crisscross the region.

Canyoning

The exhilarating sport of descending torrents and canyons by abseiling, jumping and swimming has taken off big time. Try it in the Roya valley near Saorge or in any of 70 sites in the Ubaye and Verdon valleys. There are some easier descents for beginners in the Pennafort and Destel gorges.

Abseiling down a canyon

TOP 10 WALKS

Hiking in the Mercantour

1 Vallée des Merveilles, Mercantour National Park
Only serious hikers should attempt this marvellous mountain trek. Allow 2–3 days, overnighting in refuges. Contact Park HQ before setting out *(see p114)*.

2 Blanc-Martel Trail, Verdon Gorges
A breathtaking 15-km (9-mile) trail from La Palud to Point Sublime. Allow 7–8 hours *(see p14)*.

3 Calanques, Marseille
Spectacular walking along rugged headland trails *(see p76)*.

4 Massif des Maures
The forests, valleys and peaks are covered with excellent trails *(see p91)*.

5 Coastal Path, Six-Fours-les-Plages MAP D6
The seaside walk to La Seyne starts off flat, then climbs to the Cap Sicié for fantastic views. Allow 7 hours.

6 Baou de St-Jeannet, St-Jeannet MAP G4
This stiff but rewarding walk (3–4 hours) ascends the "baou" – the rock overlooking the village near Vence.

7 Port-Cros, Îles d'Hyères
Take in a paradise of forests, creeks and headlands as you walk the coast in 5 hours *(see p50)*.

8 Dentelles de Montmirail
Trek from Sablet up to St Amand, the highest point. Six hours *(see p126)*.

9 Vieux Nice
From the Old Town up to Castle Hill and down again: the best in-town walking in the region *(see pp20–21)*.

10 Massif de l'Esterel
The very best mountain path is from Pont de l'Esterel to Mont Vinaigre. Allow 4 hours *(see p88)*.

🔟 Children's Activities

Paddling down river Sorgue

① Kayaking, Fontaine-de-Vaucluse

MAP C3 ▪ Fontaine-de-Vaucluse ▪ Kayak Vert: 04 82 29 42 42; open mid-May–mid-Oct; no credit cards

After gushing from its source at Fontaine-de-Vaucluse *(see p126)* the river Sorgue becomes idyllic, perfect for a lazy two-hour paddle downstream. Kayak Vert canoes hold two adults and two children; life jackets and return shuttle included.

② Snorkelling, Le Rayol-Canadel

The protected waters off the Var coast offer some of the best snorkelling. In summer, book a guided *sentier sous-marin* (underwater trail) session at the Domaine du Rayol *(see p54)* and spot barracudas and even octopuses.

③ Ventoux Aventure, Mormoiron

MAP C2 ▪ 920 chemin des Salettes ▪ Open Jul–Aug: daily; Sep–Jun: Wed, Sat & Sun; hours vary, check website ▪ Adm ▪ ventouxaventure.fr

Complete with zip lines, suspension bridges, a lake and a small beach, this forest adventure park has plenty to offer tree climbers aged 3 and up. Beyond the tree tops, the view of Mont Ventoux in the background is a bonus.

④ Azur Park, St-Tropez

MAP F5 ▪ Carrefour de la Foux, Gassin ▪ Open Apr–Sep ▪ Adm ▪ azurpark.fr/en

Located just outside St-Tropez, this funfair is a local institution. There are 35 attractions to choose from, including rides for toddlers. Children also adore the prehistoric mini-golf course, featuring model dinosaurs and woolly mammoths.

Aerial view of Aqualand, Fréjus

⑤ Aqualand, Fréjus

MAP F5 ▪ Quartier Le Capou, RN 98 ▪ Open mid-Jun–mid-Sep: 10am–6pm (mid Jul–Aug: to 7pm) ▪ Adm

One of the biggest water parks in Provence, this offers fun for all ages, from daredevil slides and white water thrills to calmer pools and toddler activities in the Children's Paradise.

6 Musée Oceanographique, Monaco

As well as its superb aquariums, with over 6,000 species of marine life, the Oceanographic Museum has a terrace overlooking the sea and an enclosure for African spurred turtles. The museum holds interactive exhibitions, exploring diverse marine life through the year. The 6-m (20-ft) deep aquarium gives visitors the chance to come face to face with sea turtles, sharks and giant rays (see p104).

Exhibits at Musée Oceanographique

7 Le Village des Automates, St-Cannat

MAP C4 ■ Chemin de la Dilligence ■ Open Apr–Aug: 10am–7pm daily; Sep: 10am–7pm Wed, Sat, Sun; Oct–Mar: 10am–5:30pm Wed, Sat, Sun, public & school hols

Animated automata bring storybooks to life in a series of themed tableaux, set in a wooded park. Characters include Scheherazade, Gulliver in Lilliput and Pinocchio and the whale. There's also a petting zoo, adventure park with ziplines, an elevated miniature railway, a tricycle race course as well as a massive indoor playpark.

8 Rocher Mistral, La Barben

MAP C4 ■ Route du Château ■ Open Jun–Aug: daily; Sep–early Jan & Apr–May: Fri, Sat, Sun, public & school hols ■ Closed early Jan–Mar ■ Adm ■ www.rochermistral.com

High on a hill, the striking medieval Château de la Barben (the oldest castle in Provence) and its vast grounds are the stage for immersive historical shows. Actors dressed as peasants, knights, monks and revolutionaries reenact events from the 11th century to the present day.

9 Crossbows and Catapults, Les-Baux-de-Provence

Life-sized siege engines – a ballista, catapults, trebuchets and a battering ram – bring medieval warfare to life at the dramatic fortified castle of Les Baux (see p82). Special children's activities (including training in shooting crossbows) take place during medieval festivals during the holidays and on summer weekends.

10 Les Marais du Vigueirat, Camargue

MAP B4 ■ Chemin de l'Etourneau ■ Open 9:30am–5pm daily (to 5:30pm Apr–Sep) ■ Closed Dec–mid-Jan ■ Adm

A great place for families to explore the Camargue, Vigueirat has signposted paths and nature tours for ages six and up, with the chance to see herds of white horses, black bulls, pink flamingoes, wild boar and more.

TOP 10 Places to See and Be Seen

club *(see p109)* across the Croisette from the Carlton InterContinental, one of the most luxurious seafront hotels in Cannes. Fancy cocktails and lobster rolls complement the views.

3 Le Petit Majestic, Cannes

MAP G4 ■ 6 rue Tony Allard ■ 04 93 39 94 92

This night hangout is popular with the late crowd, who party until the early hours all summer long. During the film festival *(see p68)* you'll find all the cream of the world's movie business here.

1 La Palme d'Or, Cannes

MAP G4 ■ 73 bd de la Croisette ■ 04 92 98 74 14 ■ €€€

The restaurant at the Hôtel Martinez is where stars dine, as the signed photos in the foyer attest, and the menu is suitably opulent. With two Michelin stars, the restaurant offers a fine gastronomic experience.

2 Carlton Beach Club, Cannes

Dipping your toes in the sand, soak in *la dolce vita* at this chic beach

4 Les Caves du Roy, St-Tropez

To mingle with the rich and famous, book a room at St-Trop's most stylish hotel and swan into Les Caves du Roy *(see p92)*, the hotel's nightclub. In season it's the haunt of supermodels, film stars and racing drivers. Wear your most fabulous outfit.

5 Club 55, Ramatuelle, St-Tropez

MAP F5 ■ Plage de Pampelonne, bd Patch ■ 04 94 55 55 55 ■ €€€

Ever since Le Cinquante Cinq first opened in 1955, its guest list has read like an A to Z of the rich and famous. Book ahead if you want a table in the restaurant, dress to impress and bring your platinum credit card. Open summer only.

6 Nikki Beach, Ramatuelle, St-Tropez

MAP F5 ■ 1093 chemin de l'Épi ■ 04 94 79 82 04

Join A-listers from Hollywood and Bollywood sipping on cocktails and relaxing on sun loungers to the tunes of top DJs at this glamorous beach club. Open late spring to late summer.

Carlton Beach Club, Cannes

Sun and dining terrace of the Hôtel Le Majestic Barrière, Cannes

7 Hôtel Le Majestic Barrière, Cannes

One of the flashiest café-terraces (see p110) in town attracts a high-spending, fashionable clientele year-round, and some of the world's brightest stars during the film festival – Robert De Niro, Matthew McConaughey and Jake Gyllenhaal have been sighted. Anything stronger than coffee costs a fortune.

8 Le Bistrot du Port, Golfe Juan

MAP G4 ■ 53 av des Frères Roustan ■ 04 93 63 70 64 ■ Open times vary, call to check ■ €€

The menu at this notable seafood restaurant, presided over by Mathieu Allinei, includes a great *bouillabaisse* and a variety of fish. The port itself is favoured by Hollywood stars and it is here that Napoleon I made his big, but brief comeback in 1815.

9 Le St-Paul, St-Paul-de-Vence

Nestled away in the heart of the medieval village, Le St-Paul restaurant nurtures the kind of exclusive atmosphere loved by celebrities. Beyond the elegant dining room, the walled garden terrace has tables and comfy wicker chairs surrounding a 17th-century fountain. The cuisine is creative Mediterranean (try the slow-cooked sea bass). At night, the restaurant is pure romance, illuminated by hundreds of flickering candles (see p117).

10 Hôtel du Cap-Eden-Roc, Cap d'Antibes

Book years ahead to mingle with the rich and famous at this luxurious hotel (see p143). The model for the hotel in F Scott Fitzgerald's *Tender is the Night*, it was the flagship of Riviera hedonism. The list of celebrity guests stretches back decades and includes such stars as Jennifer Lopez, Gwyneth Paltrow and Leonardo DiCaprio.

Suite at the Hôtel du Cap-Eden-Roc

For a key to restaurant price ranges see p79

🔟 Gourmet Restaurants

The grand Louis XV restaurant

1 Le Louis XV, Monte Carlo
The world's most glamorous diners expect splendour, and will get it here amid wood panelling, gilded mirrors and chandeliers (see p111). A team of top chefs takes centre stage to cook Alain Ducasse's exquisite interpretations of Provençal cuisine.

2 L'Oustau de Baumanière, Les-Baux-de-Provence
This converted farmstead (see p85) dates from the 14th century; the three-Michelin-starred food marries fresh, seasonal local produce with top-class cuisine.

3 Le Chantecler, Nice
Within the palatial Le Negresco hotel (see p143), Le Chantecler boasts Regency decor and wood panelling. The service is exquisite, as is chef Virginie Basselot's imaginative food (see p99).

4 Greenstronome, Arles
Jean-Luc Rabanel is the first eco-chef to have received two Michelin stars. His four-, six- and eight-course menus (see p85) spotlight the freshest vegetables, edible flowers and wild herbs in season.

5 La Vague d'Or, St-Tropez
At the chic beachside Cheval Blanc (see p142), chef Arnaud Donckele prepares unforgettable dishes (see p93) in a dreamy setting.

6 L'Oasis, La Napoule
In a charming Neo-Gothic villa overlooking La Napoule port, chef Nicolas Decherchi performs culinary magic. The rooftop bistro offers menus at more affordable prices.

Outdoor seating at L'Oustau de Baumanière

La Bastide de Capelongue, Bonnieux

7 La Bastide de Capelongue, Bonnieux

Young chef Noël Bérard has a growing reputation for Provençal cooking of great finesse. The surroundings are equally fine *(see p131)*.

8 La Chèvre d'Or, Èze

A Riviera legend, the "Golden Goat" combines stupendous views over the coast with exquisite, beautifully presented seasonal dishes.

9 Le Petit Nice Passedat, Marseille

Perched on a cliff overlooking the sea, this luxury hotel houses Marseille's first three-star Michelin restaurant *(see p79)*. Try beignets of sea anemones or the line-caught sea bass, followed by a delicious dark chocolate and raspberry delight.

10 La Bastide St-Antoine, Grasse

This restored 18th-century country house *(see p117)* is superbly set amid lavender and olive trees above Grasse. Equally splendid is the cooking by renowned chef Jacques Chibois.

TOP 10 REGIONAL SPECIALITIES

1 Tapenade
Purée of olives, capers, garlic and anchovies. *Anchoïade* is similar, but without capers or olives.

2 Salade Niçoise
Purists use only raw vegetables, hard-boiled eggs, anchovies, olives and olive oil, but tuna is usually added, too.

3 Olives
A signature Provençal product, olives were introduced by the Greeks in the 4th century BC, and olive oil is central to regional dishes.

4 Aïoli
Garlic mayonnaise made with olive oil. Accompanies raw vegetables, cold cod and hard-boiled eggs.

5 Pistou
Thick soup of haricot and kidney beans, pasta and other vegetables, with basil, garlic and olive oil.

6 Pieds et paquets
Lamb's feet *(pieds)* and stuffed sheep's stomach *(paquets)* in white wine.

7 Ratatouille
Stew of peppers, courgettes (zucchini), aubergines (eggplant), tomatoes and onions, sautéed in olive oil.

8 Truffles
The season for this highly flavoured, rare underground fungus runs from mid-November to mid-March. Carpentras is the centre *(see p127)*.

9 Daube
Beef (or wild boar) is marinated and slowly simmered in a sauce of red wine with herbs and garlic.

10 Bouillabaisse
Marseille fish dish of up to three species. The spicy cooking juices are served as a soup before the fish itself.

Provençal *bouillabaisse*

For a key to restaurant price ranges see p79

Vineyards and Distilleries

Château Romanin's vaulted cellar

① Château Romanin
MAP B3 ▪ Mas Romanin, St-Rémy-de-Provence ▪ 04 90 92 69 57

This stunning underground winery resembles a cathedral, and the site has had spiritual associations since the Greeks worshipped here in the 4th century BC. The owners' methods reflect this past, including cultivation by the phases of the moon.

② Château Ste-Roseline
MAP F4 ▪ 1854 route de Ste-Roseline, Les-Arcs-sur-Argens ▪ 04 94 99 50 30

This family-owned estate produces award-winning Côtes de Provence vintages. Contemporary art exhibitions are held every summer in the medieval abbey adjacent to the château and the vast grounds are lovely for walks.

③ Domaine Rabiega
MAP F4 ▪ Clos d'Ière, 516 chemin du Cros d'Aimar, Draguignan ▪ 04 94 68 44 22

Set within a wooded residential suburb, this Swedish-run domain has an innovative attitude to wine quality. The Cuvée Clos Dière is among the most expressive of Provençal wines. There is also a chic hotel and a restaurant.

④ Distilleries & Domaines de Provence
MAP D3 ▪ 9 av St-Promasse, Forcalquier ▪ www.distilleries-provence.com

Home of Henri Bardouin, the connoisseur's *pastis*. Like all *pastis*, Bardouin is based on star anise, but here they add 50 other herbs and spices, many of them local. The result is an apéritif more richly flavoured than other brands.

⑤ Domaine de Beaurenard
MAP B3 ▪ 10 av Pierre de Luxembourg, Châteauneuf-du-Pape ▪ 04 90 83 71 79

The Coulon family have been here in Provence's most famous wine village since 1695 – time enough to really perfect their skills. The Boisrenard red is the proof. They also run the region's best wine museum.

⑥ Château de Berne
MAP F4 ▪ Chemin des Imberts, Lorgues ▪ 04 94 60 43 53

British-owned Berne is the region's best wine visitors' centre. The site is picturesque, the welcome friendly, and there's a full calendar of cultural events. There are also three restaurants and a hotel on site. The best wine is the Cuvée Spéciale.

Pretty surrounds of Château de Berne

7 Château La Coste
MAP C4 ■ Rte de la Cride, Le Puy-Ste-Réparade ■ 04 42 61 89 98

Irish businessman Patrick McKillen's biodynamic vineyard features a contemporary art promenade with works by Louise Bourgeois and Tracey Emin, among others, and striking buildings by Jean Nouvel, Frank Gehry and Tadao Ando.

8 Domaine de la Citadelle
MAP C3 ■ Route de Cavaillon, Ménerbes ■ 04 90 72 41 58

Former film producer and politician Yves Rousset-Rouard sunk a fortune into this stylish set-up. The Côtes de Luberon wines are treated with respect, and the on-site Corkscrew Museum is unique.

Domaine de la Citadelle

9 Domaine St André de Figuière
MAP E5 ■ BP47, Quartier St Honoré, La Londe-les-Maures ■ 04 94 00 44 70

In a superb location, set back from the sea and next to a bird sanctuary, Alain Combard and his family make wines of great finesse. Note that the visitors' entrance to the cellar is round the back of a steel tank.

10 Château de Pibarnon
MAP D5 ■ 410 chemin de la Croix des Signaux, La Cadière-d'Azur ■ 04 94 90 12 73

Perched directly above the sea, this may be the most attractively sited wine château in Provence. Father and son Henri and Eric have wrestled the unyielding land to produce delicious red wines now in the forefront of the Bandol appellation.

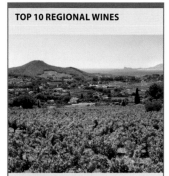

TOP 10 REGIONAL WINES

Vineyards in Bandol

1 Bandol
The home of the Mourvèdre grape produces fine and vigorous reds.

2 Châteauneuf-du-Pape
At their best, the reds are dark and powerful, while the (rarer) whites are intensely fruity.

3 Beaumes de Venise
France's richest fortified dessert wine, made from the Muscat grape.

4 Côtes-de-Provence
Famed for rosés, this region is now also producing classy reds and heady whites.

5 Gigondas
Sometimes known as "son of Châteauneuf-du-Pape" but the full-bodied wines definitely stand out on their own.

6 Côteaux d'Aix-en-Provence
Fast-improving red and rosé wines.

7 Cassis
Fresh, dry whites – particularly good served with Provençal fish dishes.

8 Côtes du Ventoux
The reds, especially, can be very rewarding – although rosés are great for summer picnics.

9 Côtes du Luberon
Another hugely improved group of wines, not least due to investment from fashionable outsiders.

10 Côtes du Rhône Villages
In theory, one step up from ordinary Côtes du Rhône, but they can be several steps up in practice – especially if the name of the village (such as Cairanne) is mentioned on the label.

⏉ Provence for Free

Exhibition at Villa Arson, Nice

① Contemporary Culture
MAP N1 ■ 20 av Stephen Liegeard, Nice ■ 04 92 07 73 73 ■ Open 2–6pm (Jul & Aug: to 7pm) Wed–Mon (during exhibitions only) ■ www.villa-arson.org

The Villa Arson is a fine art school and contemporary art gallery housed in a bucolic villa in northern Nice. Visitors can enjoy a changing roster of exhibitions focusing on contemporary French sculpture, Parisian Pop Art and video montages.

② Pedalling Provence
Many hotels offer free bike loan for their guests (see p135). The region's larger cities, such as Marseille, Aix and Avignon, also have inexpensive bike share schemes.

③ Vineyard Tastings
Vines have carpeted Provence and the Côte d'Azur since Roman times. Almost every vineyard offers free tastings to visitors amid bucolic grounds – although buying at least a bottle (at bargain château prices) is considered polite. Even the region's finest vintners (see pp60–61) welcome visitors.

④ Food for Free
MAP B3 ■ pl Pie, Avignon ■ 04 90 27 15 15 ■ www.avignon-leshalles.com/la-petite-cuisine-des-halles

Every Saturday morning at 11am, one of Avignon's leading chefs cooks up a storm in the city's Les Halles food market. La Petite Cuisine des Halles' programme promises complimentary tastings, recipes and all sorts of culinary tips and techniques.

⑤ Church Art
For centuries the Catholic church was the most powerful economic force in Provence, and it shows in the masterpieces on its walls: visit, for example, Grasse's Notre-Dame-du-Puy (see p40), where a Fragonard and a trio of Rubens canvases adorn the interior. But you can see works of interest by the Old Masters for free in almost every church and cathedral in the region.

⑥ Lavender Fields
Blooming lavender fields are best seen from June to early August. Some of the prettiest sights can be seen while driving through Castellet, Gordes, Sault and Forcalquier. The hillside town of Sault draws crowds during its Fête de la Lavande, which is held on 15 August.

Lavender fields in bloom, Provence

St-Jean-Cap-Ferrat

7 Walk the World's Wealthiest Peninsula

MAP H4

Cap-Ferrat is the world's second-priciest property spot (only Monaco is more expensive). A 6-km (4-mile) public footpath makes its way round the cape, past billionaires' gardens from Plage de Passable beach in Villefranche to David Niven's former home near St-Jean.

8 St-Tropez on a Shoestring

Little comes cheap in Europe's A-list getaway. But while the celebs soak up the sun at exclusive Plage de Pampelonne beach bars such as Club 55 (see p58), the rest of the shore is free to mere mortals. And Le Café on place des Lices (see p25) offers guests free use of *pétanque* balls.

9 A Princely View of Monaco

Peer out from the palatial mound of Monte Carlo (see p103) on a sunny day to glimpse Corsica twinkling in the distance. Whatever the weather, you can see the daily Changing of the Palace Guard.

10 In the Footsteps of Cézanne

Aix-en-Provence's most famous inhabitant is cemented into history with a walking trail (see p18). Follow the brass floor plaques (with an accompanying leaflet if you wish) that lead you through Cézanne's favourite haunts around town.

TOP 10 BUDGET TIPS

1 A hotel *petit déjeuner* (breakfast) can cost you upwards of €10. Hit a café for fresh croissants instead, but take note: a *café-crème* or *café au lait* is coffee for tourists. Locals sip *un express* (espresso) instead.

2 Hitchhiking is permitted on all roads except *autoroutes* (motorways).

3 Local wine by the *pichet*, or half-litre carafe, will halve your drinks bill. It's also acceptable, when dining, to ask for a *carafe d'eau* (jug of tap water) rather than a bottle of mineral water.

4 Museum passes are a steal. The French Riviera Pass grants free access and discounts to several sites in Nice and along the Côte d'Azur. Students and over-60s often qualify for a discount, and state-owned museums are free to EU students under 26 (ID is required).

5 Book TGV tickets online at *www.oui.sncf* for discounts – such as Nice to Avignon from €20. Rail passes are great value too.

6 Hotel chains hotelF1 and B&B Hotels offer bargain, no-frills rooms.

7 City-centre self-catering apartments work out far cheaper than hotels for families staying a few days. The countryside alternatives are *gîtes*.

8 Youth hostels (no age limit) may be found in most major cities and in many national parks. Provençal campsites are not much cheaper than a budget hotel. Wild camping is discouraged.

9 Provençal markets can supply all you need for the perfect seaside picnic at less than the cost of a café terrace snack.

10 Sign up online for one of the region's many city bike share schemes. Nice's VéloBleu and Marseille's Le Vélo offer bicycles from €1 per hour.

VéloBleu shared bikes in Nice

Festivals and Events

(1) Festival de Quatuors à Cordes
MAP E5–F5 ■ **Feb**

Flower-bedecked floats, accompanied by live music, are paraded through villages throughout the Var. Among the main corsos are those in St-Raphaël and Ste-Maxime.

(2) Nice Carnival
MAP H4 ■ **Feb**

Over 16 days in February, Nice goes wild as multicoloured floats, carnival figures and performing troupes take to the streets. Europe's liveliest event also features the Battle of the Flowers.

Carnival figure in the parade at Nice

(3) Cannes Film Festival
MAP G4 ■ **May**

Some 30,000 film professionals attend this world-famous gathering, to do business and, incidentally, see a few films. The atmosphere is glamorously electric. As a member of the public, don't expect to meet, or even see, the stars, except as they mount the steps of the Festival Palace for a screening.

(4) Fête de la Transhumance, St Rémy-de-Provence
MAP B3 ■ **Whitsun weekend**

Upwards of 3,000 sheep, as well as goats and donkeys, accompanied by shepherds in traditional costume with sheep dogs, cram into the old village, for a sheep drive (transhumance) to upland pastures.

Performer at the Avignon Festival

(5) Avignon Festival
MAP B3 ■ **Jul**

France's greatest theatre event is really two festivals. The official one takes over the Papal Palace's Courtyard of Honour (see p12) and other venues for both modern and classical drama. However, it is the unofficial "off" festival which enlivens the town, with street performers and up to 400 shows a day, from dance to burlesque comedy.

(6) Aix Festival
MAP C4 ■ **Jul**

Founded in 1948, this is a great lyrical event. As well as classical opera in the courtyard of the Archbishop's Palace and other venues, there are more contemporary works, recitals by musicians, music masterclasses at its Académie Européenne de Musique and street theatre.

(7) Nice Jazz Festival
MAP Q3 ■ **Jul**

Founded in 1948, the best of the region's many jazz festivals draws

Musician at the Nice Jazz Festival

some of the biggest names in the music business. The festival sees 32 concerts over 6 nights on two stages in Place Masséna, one concentrating on jazz and the other mixing world music, pop and other genres.

8 Chorégies d'Orange
MAP B2 ▪ Jul

France's oldest music festival, dating from 1869, has the town's Roman theatre as its main venue *(see p125)*. The original stage wall ensures perfect acoustics for the classical operas that have earned the event an international reputation.

Chorégies d'Orange show

9 International Piano Festival, La Roque d'Anthéron
MAP C4 ▪ Mid-Jul–mid-Aug

Since 1980, the festival has drawn the cream of the world's classical and jazz pianists to play beneath the plane trees and the night sky at Château de Florans, located in the charming village of La Roque d'Anthéron.

10 Fête de la Véraison, Châteauneuf-du-Pape
MAP B3 ▪ 1st weekend Aug

Take a step back in time to celebrate the ripening of grapes with villagers dressed in historic costume. Parades, performances and demonstrations of medieval crafts take place over three days of festivities.

TOP 10 SPORTING EVENTS

Monaco Grand Prix

1 Paris to Nice "Race to the Sun"
MAP H4 ▪ Mar
Watch the final leg of the international cycling year's first major race.

2 Monte Carlo Tennis Masters
MAP H3 ▪ Apr
One of the tennis circuit's more prestigious events.

3 Olympic Sailing Week, Hyères
MAP E6 ▪ Apr
Some 1,000 boats from 50 nations compete in this sailing event.

4 Monaco Grand Prix
MAP H3 ▪ May
The one and only street race on the Formula One calendar.

5 Joûtes Provençales, St Mandrier-sur-Mer
MAP G4 ▪ Jun
An unusual sporting event centred on waterborne jousting.

6 Verdon Canyon Challenge
MAP E3 ▪ Jun
Tough races of 8–100 km (5–62 miles) through this dramatic scenery.

7 Pétanque World Championships, Marseille
MAP K4 ▪ Jul
Four days of boules, culminating in a final on the Vieux Port.

8 Feria du Riz, Arles
MAP B4 ▪ Sep
Bullfighting and other festivities welcome the Camargue rice harvest.

9 Les Voiles de St-Tropez
MAP F5 ▪ Sep–Oct
Six-day regatta for both traditional and modern sailing boats.

10 Olympique de Marseille
The favourite French football team *(see p76)* plays home games July to May.

🔟 Offshore Islands

View from Port-Cros, one of the Îles d'Hyères

1 Port-Cros, Îles d'Hyères

A national park *(see p50)*, the smallest and most mountainous of the Hyères isles is dense with pine woods and oaks. Paths lead up to clifftops offering dramatic views. For relaxation, La Palud is by far the best beach.

2 Le Levant, Îles d'Hyères

MAP F6 ▪ Ferry from Hyères

Although 90 per cent of this island is a French Navy missile base, the other 10 per cent is a naturist colony. Clothes must be worn at the port and in administrative buildings.

3 Îles du Frioul

MAP C5 ▪ Ferry from Vieux Port, Marseille

The linked islands of Ratonneau and Pomègues guard Marseille harbour *(see p75)*. Beyond Port Frioul, white rocks ruggedly conceal unspoiled little beaches. The diving and snorkelling here is renowned.

4 Île d'If

MAP C5 ▪ Ferry from Vieux Port, Marseille

This prison island is most famous as the place from which Dumas' fictional Count of Monte Cristo escaped *(see p41)*. You may even visit the "Count's dungeon".

5 Ste-Marguerite, Îles de Lérins

MAP G4 ▪ Ferry from Cannes harbour

Ste-Marguerite offers woods of pine and eucalyptus and stony coves. In 1687, the Man in the Iron Mask was imprisoned in the fort *(see p46)* here.

6 Porquerolles, Îles d'Hyères

MAP E6 ▪ Ferry from La Tour-Fondue, near Giens

The largest of the French Riviera islands is the car-free hideaway of Porquerolles. Hire a bike or explore on foot to appreciate this paradise of vineyards, olive groves, scented forests and glorious beaches.

Tranquil beach in Porquerolles

7 Îles des Embiez
MAP D6 ▪ Ferry from Le Brusc, near Six-Fours-les-Plages ▪ www.lesilespaulricard.com

The larger of two islands developed for tourism by drinks magnate Paul Ricard, Les Embiez is a delight. Development has been sensitively merged into the landscape, leaving most of the island's creeks, woods and salt marshes untouched.

8 St-Honorat, Îles de Lérins
MAP G4 ▪ 04 92 99 54 00 ▪ Ferry from Cannes ▪ Fortified monastery: Closed for renovation until further notice ▪ www.abbayedelerins.com

St-Honorat has been run by monks almost continually since the 5th century. It has several 10th-century chapels and an impressive 11th-century monastery. You can stroll through the vineyards, cultivated by the monks, and buy the wine from the shop.

St-Honorat's fortified monastery

9 Île de Bendor
MAP D5 ▪ Ferry from Bandol

With a tiny harbour and beaches, this island too has been developed by Paul Ricard and is smaller than Îles des Embiez. But the tourist development is as sensitive as on Les Embiez, and complements the natural landscape.

10 Île Verte
MAP D5 ▪ Ferry from Vieux Port, La Ciotat

The "Verte" of its name refers to the island's greenery, notably the trees topping the steep cliffs. Billed as "one of the last virgin islands of the Mediterranean coast", the islet has tiny creeks and beaches.

TOP 10 ISLAND ACTIVITIES

Cycling on Porquerolles

1 Cycling
On Porquerolles and Les Embiez, cycle the forest paths to creeks and beaches.

2 Snorkelling, Port-Cros
National Park Office ▪ 04 94 12 82 30 ▪ www.portcrosparcnational.fr
Follow a signposted underwater "nature trail" from La Palud.

3 Fort Ste-Agathe, Porquerolles
04 94 58 07 24 ▪ Open mid-May–mid-Oct; check website for times of guided tours ▪ Adm ▪ www.porquerolles.com
Exhibitions on the region's nature.

4 Diving, Île des Embiez
Centre de Plongée ▪ 06 87 61 03 20
Courses in water rich with marine life.

5 Lighthouse Walk, Porquerolles
A 90-minute round trip to one of the finest lighthouses.

6 Fort de l'Estissac, Port-Cros
Open Jun–Sep: 11am–1pm & 3–5pm
Exhibits on local history.

7 Aquascope, Île des Embiez
Open Apr–Oct ▪ 06 23 36 39 55 ▪ Adm
A glass "bubble" over water allows close encounters of a marine kind.

8 Sailing and Sea Kayaking, Bandol
Société Nautique de Bandol ▪ www.sn-bandol.com
Hire and classes in summer.

9 Vallon de la Solitude Walk, Port-Cros
A two-hour walk through shady forest to the Fort de la Vigie.

10 Museum of Wine and Spirits, Île de Bendor
Open mid-Jun–mid-Sep: 1–6pm Thu–Tue ▪ www.lesilespaulricard.com
A display of 8,000 bottles from over 50 countries.

Provence and the Côte d'Azur Area by Area

The perched village of Les-Baux-de-Provence, Bouches-du-Rhône

📐 Marseille

The oldest city in France was founded 2,600 years ago by Greek settlers from Asia Minor, and it has barely seen a quiet moment since. Open-hearted and tumultuous, it is backed by chalk hills and flanked by white cliffs, with its face to the sea. The sea is Marseille's

Ceiling of Notre-Dame de la Garde

raison d'être, making it a trading hub and entry point for immigrants. As a result, Marseille is a collection of urban villages, from the souk-like market areas to tiny fishing ports. But all its citizens are *Marseillais*: loud, rebellious and volatile. This is the home of French music, football and *bouillabaisse*. Picaresque and picturesque, it's a place in which to feel alive.

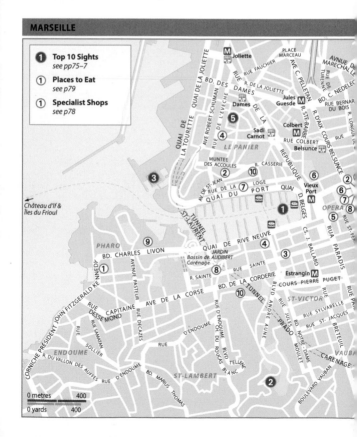

MARSEILLE

- **1** Top 10 Sights *see pp75–7*
- **1** Places to Eat *see p79*
- **1** Specialist Shops *see p78*

Marseille's charming Vieux Port

① Vieux Port
MAP K4

Commercial sea traffic might have moved round the corner to newer docks in the 19th century, but the old port remains the heart of city life. Bobbing with boats and fringed with restaurants, it's where the *Marseillais* gather for festivities and

to buy fish. The occupying Nazis tried to subdue the city by blowing up the north side of the port in 1943, but Marseille's indomitable nature won the day.

② Notre-Dame de la Garde
MAP K6 ■ Rue Fort du Sanctuaire ■ Open 7am–6pm daily

This Romanesque-Byzantine church is the symbol of Marseille. Perched on the highest hill and topped by a gold statue of the Virgin, it can be seen from everywhere in the city. Built in the 1850s and restored in the early 2000s, its vaulted crypt is carved out of the rock.

Contemporary interior of MuCEM

③ Museum of Civilizations of Europe and the Mediterranean (MuCEM)
MAP J4 ■ 7 prom Robert Laffont ■ Open Nov–Apr: 10am–6pm Wed–Mon (May–Jun & Sep–Oct: to 7pm; Jul–Aug: to 8pm) ■ Adm

This museum is split between a striking postmodernist building on the seafront and the adjacent Fort St-Jean. It features art from around the Mediterranean, from Neolithic times to the present day.

Palais Longchamp fountains

4 Palais Longchamp
MAP M2 ■ Bd Jardin Zoo-logique ■ Museums: open 9am–6pm Tue–Sun; closed public hols; adm for temporary exhibitions (free first Sun of the month)

Longchamp is the greatest expression of Marseille's 19th-century "golden age". What is essentially a water tower is embellished in palatial Second Empire style with fountains, columns and animal sculptures. The central gallery is flanked by two ornate wings, home to the Fine Arts and Natural History museums.

5 Le Panier and Vieille Charité
MAP J3 ■ La Vieille Charité: 2 rue de la Charité ■ Open 9am–6pm Tue–Sun ■ Closed 1 Jan, 1 May,1 Nov, 25 Dec; ■ Adm

Wriggling up the hill north of the Vieux Port, Le Panier is Marseille's oldest sector. This is where the Greeks settled and, later, where the city's immigrants began their new lives. The streets are alive with different cultures. La Vieille Charité, the 17th-century workhouse and now a cultural centre, houses the museums of Mediterranean Archaeology and of contemporary art. The domed central chapel is Italian Baroque at its purest.

6 Musée Grobet-Labadié
MAP M3 ■ 140 bd Longchamp ■ Open 9am–6pm Tue–Sun ■ Closed 1 Jan, 1 May, 1 & 11 Nov, 25 Dec ■ Adm

Opposite the Palais Longchamp, this museum is set in the former private mansion of a rich 19th-century art-loving Marseille family. Its original decor has been retained, recreating bourgeois life at the peak of the city's prosperity. Walls are hung with a unique collection of Gobelin and Aubusson tapestries, while the salons boast sculpture, paintings, drawings and furniture from the 13th to the 19th centuries.

Painting at Musée Grobet-Labadié

7 Prado Beaches
MAP C5

Around the corniche from the Vieux Port, past the picturesque fishing port of Vallon des Auffes to the start of the *calanques*, stretch Marseille's boldly modern beaches. They were reclaimed from the sea with earth excavated during the building of the city's metro system. On summer days, they feature every conceivable beach sporting activity; at night, the Escale Borély beach area offers some of the town's trendiest nightspots.

8 Les Calanques
MAP C5

Within 15 minutes' drive of the city centre you are out of town and into

---

THE FOOTBALL CAPITAL

Champions of Europe, then enmeshed in match-fixing scandals: the recent history of the Olympique de Marseille football team has matched the turbulence of its home town. But this has done nothing to dissuade the fans of the most popular French team – football is the lifeblood of Marseille, the Stade Vélodrome its place of worship.

a different world. White rocks plunge into the blue sea and the road winds into inlets *(calanques)* of great beauty *(see p52)*. This is where the *Marseillais* spend their weekends, eating, drinking and keeping rich developers out. After Les Goudes, access to even more picturesque creeks (towards Cassis) is by foot or boat only.

Imposing walls of the Château d'If

⑨ Château d'If
MAP C5 ■ Open Apr–Sep: 10:30am–6pm daily; Oct–Mar: 10:30am–5:15pm Tue–Sun ■ Ferry from Vieux Port ■ Adm

This offshore island fortress was built in the 16th century to protect the city's port and was turned into a prison in 1634. Among its inmates were the real Comte de Mirabeau, and Alexandre Dumas' *(see p45)* fictional Count of Monte Cristo.

⑩ Musée des Arts Décoratifs, de la Faïence et de la Mode
MAP C5 ■ 134 av Clot Bey ■ Open 9am–6pm Tue–Sun ■ Closed 1 Jan, 1 May, 1 & 11 Nov, 25 Dec ■ Adm

Château Borély, a masterpiece of 18th-century architecture, houses exhibition space devoted to decorative arts and furniture; earthenware, ceramics and glass; and fashion from the 17th century to the present day. It brings together collections formerly scattered between the Musée de la Faïence, the Musée Cantini and the Musée du Vieux Marseille, along with the furniture collection of the Château itself. The gardens host outdoor exhibitions and concerts.

A MORNING EXPLORING MARSEILLE

▶ Start your day off at the lush Parc Longchamp (metro Cinq Avenues-Longchamp) for a stroll through the gardens, zoo or the museums of the **Palais Longchamp**, and perhaps also the **Musée Grobet-Labadié**, just across from the park entrance.

From here you can walk towards the centre on the leafy boulevard Longchamp (or better yet take the very stylish and popular T2 tram) to boulevard Garibaldi; walk one block south to rue du Marché des Capucins, colourful heart of the city's souk market area (also known as the Marché de Noailles; closed Sun).

When you're done with browsing, follow this street eastwards and turn right into cours Julien, a lively centre for musicians and artists, full of alternative bars and street art. From the end of the street, take rue d'Aubagne north and then left into rue Estelle. Here the style heats up quickly, with the designer shops in and around rue St-Ferréol.

Soon after rue Estelle becomes rue Grignan, visit the **Musée Cantini** *(open 10am–6pm Tue–Sun; closed public hols; adm)*, which houses a magnificent modernist collection of Fauvist, Cubist and Surrealist paintings.

Rue Paradis brings you to the **Vieux Port** *(see p75)*. End your morning stroll along place Thiars, a hive of galleries, restaurants and bars. Enjoy a sumptuous meal at **Les Trois Forts** at boulevard Charles Livon *(see p79)*.

See map on pp74–5 ◀

Specialist Shops

1 L'Épicerie Idéal
MAP L4 ■ **11 rue d'Aubagne**

Located in the neighbourhood of Noailles, famous as "the belly of Marseille", this deli-restaurant has irresistible selections of cheeses, cold meats, wines and much more.

2 Maison Empereur
MAP L4 ■ **4 rue des Récolettes**
■ **Closed Sun** ■ **www.empereur.fr**

France's oldest hardware shop, founded in 1827, is a quirky institution. It sells kitchen and household goods, leather, toys and much more.

The quirky Maison Empereur

3 Casablanca
MAP L4 ■ **63 cours Julien**
■ **www.boutiquecasablanca.com**

One of the arbiters of trendy Marseille style, featuring colourful, comfortable women's clothing.

4 La Maison de la Boule
MAP J3 ■ **4 pl des 13 Cantons**

As well as showcasing the history of pétanque, this delightful shop sells everything you need to enjoy this Provençal sport.

5 La Chocolatière de Marseille
MAP K4 ■ **35 rue Vacon**

This tiny establishment makes the best chocolate in the city. Specialities include the mouthwatering *Barre Marseillaise*, made in a wide range of flavours, such as orange and praline.

6 Galeries Lafayette
MAP K4
■ **Centre Commercial Bourse**

The largest store in town is a one-stop shop (clothes, gifts, wines, groceries and more) for those with less time to spare.

7 L'Herboristerie du Père Blaize
MAP L4 ■ **4 et 6 rue Méolan et du Père Blaize**

This traditional herbalist shop, with wooden cabinets full of dried plants and flowers, has been run by the same family for six generations.

8 Le Four des Navettes
MAP J5 ■ **136 rue Sainte**

The oldest bakery in town and, since 1781, home of the traditional Marseillais *navette*, a small biscuit (cookie) flavoured with orange blossom and shaped like a boat.

9 Dromel Aîné
MAP L6 ■ **19 av Prado**

Even older than the above, Dromel Aîné has been in the business of selling fantastic chocolates, sweets, and a range of unusual teas and coffees since 1760.

10 La Compagnie de Provence
MAP J4 ■ **1 rue Caisserie**

Not far from the Vieux Port, this shop sells authentic olive oil *savon de Marseille* in all its forms, plus scented candles and diffusers.

La Compagnie de Provence

Places to Eat

> **PRICE CATEGORIES**
> For a three-course meal for one with half a bottle of wine (or equivalent meal), taxes and extra charges.
> ....
> € under €40 ■ €€ €40–€60 ■ €€€ over €60

Plateau de fruits de mer at Chez Toinou

Restaurant Chez Michel
MAP J5 ■ 6 rue des Catalans
■ 04 91 52 30 63 ■ €€€

Chez Michel is known for serving the finest *bouillabaisse* in town, as well as several other traditional Marseillaise seafood specialities. It overlooks Catalan beach.

2 Dayo
MAP J4 ■ 40 rue Caisserie
■ 04 91 93 13 37 ■ Closed Sun, Mon ■ €

This a favourite with locals and visitors alike for its delicious seafood and steaks grilled on the *plancha*.

3 Les Arcenaulx
MAP K5 ■ 25 cours Honoré d'Estienne d'Orves ■ 04 91 59 80 30 ■ Closed Sun ■ €€€

Dine in the extraordinary setting of a former 17th-century arsenal, complete with atmospheric vaults. Besides the regional restaurant, there is a bookshop and a boutique.

4 La Table du Fort
MAP K5 ■ 8 rue Fort Notre Dame ■ 04 91 33 97 65 ■ Closed Sat L, Mon L, Tue L ■ €€

A welcoming husband-and-wife team consistently serve inventive contemporary cuisine made using local produce. The restaurant is just a few steps from the Vieux Port.

5 Le Petit Nice Passedat
Anse de Maldormé, Corniche J F Kennedy ■ 04 91 59 25 92 ■ Closed Sun & Mon ■ €€€

Highly awarded, elegant fish and seafood restaurant in a luxury hotel (run by French chef Gerald Passedat) with glorious sea views.

6 Chez Toinou
MAP L4 ■ 3 cours St Louis ■ 04 91 33 14 94 ■ Closed Sun, Mon ■ €€

One of the best – and cheapest – places for seafood in Marseille. Those willing to share can savour a *plateau de fruits de mer* for about €21 per person; for a simpler option, try the mussels and chips.

7 Le Souk
MAP J4 ■ 98 quai du Port ■ 04 91 91 29 29 ■ Closed Mon ■ €

Great Moroccan food in a lovely setting with a view of the cathedral.

8 La Mercerie
MAP L4 ■ 9 cours St-Louis ■ 04 91 06 18 44 ■ Closed Mon L, Tue, Wed, Thu L ■ €€

This restaurant with a buzzy vibe is run by a young trio serving creative neo-bistro dishes and natural wines.

9 Les Trois Forts
MAP J5 ■ Hôtel Sofitel du Vieux-Port, 36 bd Charles-Livon ■ 04 91 15 59 56 ■ €€€

Great views over the port accompany sumptuous seafood dishes.

10 Sépia
MAP K5 ■ 2 rue Vauvenargues ■ 09 83 82 67 27 ■ Closed Sun, Mon ■ €€

Sépia serves delicious meals made from the freshest market produce.

See map on pp74–5 ←

🔟 Bouches-du-Rhône

The Bouches-du-Rhône region is aptly named (*bouches* means mouths), for here the river splits into several separate streams, flowing into the Mediterranean via the lagoons and grassy plains of the Camargue. The Rhône marks Provence's western boundary and for centuries it was the region's highway. Many important towns grew up along its banks, while villages and medieval abbeys nestle in the hills. Windswept beaches fringe the Camargue, but east of the delta the coast becomes rocky, with small inlets (*calanques*).

Flamingoes in the Camargue

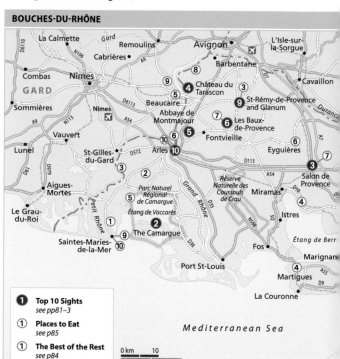

BOUCHES-DU-RHÔNE

🔟 **Top 10 Sights**
   see pp81–3

① **Places to Eat**
   see p85

① **The Best of the Rest**
   see p84

Mediterranean Sea

0 km   10

0 miles   10

Algiers ✈   Tunis ✈

and animal species, is protected within the Parc Naturel Régional de Camargue (see pp26–7) and other conservation areas.

Fountain in Aix-en-Provence

① Aix-en-Provence

Aix (see pp18–19) is a stone's throw from the sprawl of Marseille, but keeps its own identity, with cosmopolitan cafés, a grand cathedral and beautiful 18th-century fountains.

② The Camargue

This vast expanse of wetlands, salt marshes, lagoons and grazing land, home to a range of rare bird

③ Salon de Provence
MAP C4

Salon, one of the oldest villages in Provence, is today a busy modern town, host to the French Air Force training school. The old town, sitting on a hill, has an attractive historic centre, with medieval buildings, quiet streets and leafy, café-lined squares. The main attraction is the Château de l'Empéri (see p84) dating from the 10th century. Other places to visit include the small museum dedicated to Nostradamus, who lived here in the 16th century, and the Musée de Savon at Savonnerie Fabre, which bears witness to the olive oil industry which has existed here for over 600 years.

Château de Tarascon

④ Château de Tarascon
MAP B3 ▪ Bd du Roi René, Tarascon ▪ Open Jan–Mar & Oct–Dec: 9:30am–12:30pm & 2–5pm Tue–Sun; Apr: 9:30am–12:30pm & 2–5pm daily; May–Sep: 9:30am–12:30pm & 1:45–6:30pm daily ▪ Closed public hols ▪ Adm

The pale battlements of the Château de Tarascon were built to guard a vital Rhône crossing on Provence's borders; the castle has steep, crenellated curtain walls between massive round towers. It was begun by King Louis of Anjou, ruler of Provence in the 15th century, and was completed by his successor, King René. On his death, Provence became part of France (see p37) and the castle served as a prison until 1926.

5 Abbaye de Montmajour

MAP B4 ■ Rte de Fontvieille, Arles ■ Open May: 10am–5pm daily; Jun–Sep: 10am–6:30pm daily; Oct–Apr: 10am–5pm Tue–Sun ■ Closed 1 Jan, 1 May, 1 & 11 Nov, 25 Dec ■ Adm

This massive, fortress-like abbey was built by Benedictine monks in the 10th century (see p47). Then, the low hill on which it stands was an island surrounded by marshes and is still known as Mount Ararat. Damaged by fire in 1726, it was restored in the 19th century, and its Église Notre-Dame is one of the largest Romanesque buildings in Provence. Below the church, a 12th-century crypt and chapel have been carved into the hillside.

Château and harbour of Cassis

7 Cassis

MAP D5

This pretty fishing port (see p49) with its brightly coloured boats anchored in a harbour on a rugged, rocky coastline, was a favourite with painters such as Dufy, Derain and Matisse (see pp44–5). All of them were inspired by its clear light and Mediterranean hues. Amazingly, it has escaped being spoiled by tourism. Cassis is also noted for its excellent seafood (fresh sea urchins are considered a local delicacy).

Abbaye de Montmajour

6 Les-Baux-de-Provence

MAP B4 ■ Château des Baux: open daily; Mar, Oct: 9:30am–6pm; Apr–Jun, Sep: 9am–7pm; Jul, Aug: 9am–7:30pm; Nov–Feb: 10am–5pm; adm

Perched on a limestone crag, Les Baux is one of the most dramatic fortified villages in Provence (see p48). It is crowned by a ruined château with walls that date from the 10th century. Église St-Vincent has 20th-century stained glass by Max Ingrand.

8 Abbaye de Silvacane

MAP C4 ■ La Roque d'Anthéron ■ Open Apr–May: 10am–12:30pm & 2–5pm Tue–Sun; Jun–Sep: 10am–12:30pm & 2–5:45pm daily; Oct–Mar: 10am–12:30pm & 2–4:45pm Tue–Sun ■ Adm

Along with Sénanque (see pp30–31) and Thoronet, Silvacane is one of the three great sister-abbeys built in the 12th century by the Cistercian order as it rose to prominence in Provence. Its plain, austere architecture reflects the rule of the order, which was founded by St Bernard in protest of the luxury and corruption of other monasteries. The church has a high, vaulted transept and the cloister arcades and refectory were added in the 13th and 14th centuries. Abandoned by its monks in the late 14th century, it became a living abbey once again in the 20th century.

BLACK BULLS AND WHITE HORSES

The wild black bulls of the Camargue are one of the symbols of Bouches-du-Rhône, along with white horses – direct descendants of the prehistoric wild horse of Europe. These are still ridden by *gardians*, the sombrero-wearing cowboys of the Camargue.

LITTLE ROME: A MORNING IN ARLES

⑨ St Rémy-de-Provence and Glanum

MAP B3 ■ Musée des Alpilles: pl Favier, St-Rémy; open May–Oct: 10am–6pm Tue–Sun; Nov–Apr: 1–5:30pm Tue–Sat; closed 1 Jan, 1 May, 24–26 Dec; adm

Overlooked by the wooded, limestone hills of Les Alpilles, St-Rémy is a perfect exploring base. Mansions built in the 15th and 16th centuries grace its historic centre. One of them was the original home of the de Sade family, ancestors of the notorious Marquis. It houses the small Musée des Alpilles, displaying artifacts found at Glanum, about 30 minutes' walk from the town centre. Here, the site of one of the most ancient Greek-Roman settlements in Provence (see p39) is marked by a magnificent triumphal arch and mausoleum.

⑩ Roman Arles

The delightful town of Arles (see pp16–17), founded by the Romans, stands on the east bank of the Rhône and is the gateway to Provence from the west.

Les Arènes, Arles

⏵ Start the day with a visit to the largest and most striking Roman monument in Provence, **Les Arènes** (see p16). From the highest tier of seats you have a fine view of the historic centre and the Rhône. From here, walk across to the **Théâtre Antique** (see p16), for another glimpse of Roman Arles, then walk down the rue du Cloître to the place de la République, where water gushes from bronze masks at the foot of an obelisk, brought here from Egypt by the Romans.

On the east side of the square, visit the fine Romanesque **Église St-Trophime** (see p16), with its sculpted pillars crowned with little figures of saints and martyrs. Follow the rue de l'Hôtel de Ville to **Les Thermes de Constantin** (see p16), the remains of a palace built for a 4th-century AD Roman emperor. Then spend up to an hour in the **Musée Réattu** (rue du Grand-Prieuré; open Tue–Sun; adm), with its fine collection of art from the 18th to 20th centuries, including works by Picasso.

Another great painter, Van Gogh, is associated with Place du Forum, which is cluttered with cafés – one has been painted to look just as it was in his work *Terrasse du Café le Soir*. Stop in for coffee. End the morning at the **Fondation Vincent van Gogh Arles** (35 rue du Dr Fanton; open Apr–Oct: 10am–6pm daily; Nov–Mar: 11am–6pm Tue–Sun; adm), with works by contemporaries highlighting Van Gogh's influence on 20th- and 21st-century artists.

The Best of the Rest

Parc Ornithologique du Pont-de-Gau, the Camargue

MAP A4 ■ Open 9am–6pm daily; park entrance: open sunrise–sunset ■ Adm

For a superb view of the Camargue, visit the park (see p27), where enclosures display the lagoons' bird life.

2 Musée de la Camargue

MAP B4 ■ Mas du Pont de Rousty, Arles ■ Open Apr–Sep: 9am–5:30pm daily; Oct–Mar: 10am–5pm daily ■ Closed weekends in Nov–Jan, 1 Jan, 25 Dec ■ Adm

The Camargue comes to life in this fascinating museum (see p26).

3 Maison du Riz, Albaron

MAP A4 ■ Mas de la Vigne ■ 06 31 03 40 11 ■ Open by appt Apr–Nov: 9:30am–12:30pm & 2–6pm Sun–Fri ■ Adm

Set amid Camargue paddy fields close to the Petit Rhône, this rice museum is run by the third and fourth generations of a family of rice farmers.

4 Pont Flavien

MAP B4

A Roman bridge from Augustus' reign in the 1st century AD, Pont Flavien (see p39) has beautifully preserved triumphal arches at both ends.

5 Château de Beaucaire

MAP B3 ■ Pl Raimond VII ■ 04 66 59 26 57 ■ Open mid-Oct–Mar: 10am–5pm Wed–Sun; Apr–Jun & Sep–mid-Oct: 9:30am–6pm Wed–Sun; Jul–Aug: 9:30am–6pm daily

This ruined 11th-century castle faces the Château de Tarascon (see p81).

6 Eyguières

MAP C4

This village was the source of Arles' water supply in Roman times. A 12th-century chapel, a 17th-century church and a ruined castle stand here.

7 Château de l'Empéri, Salon-de-Provence

MAP C4 ■ Montée du Puech ■ Open 10am–12:30pm & 2–6pm Tue–Sun ■ Closed public hols ■ Adm

This imposing 9th-century château was once the seat of the archbishops of Arles. It now houses a fascinating museum of military history.

8 Abbaye St-Michel de Frigolet

MAP B3 ■ Open 8am–6pm daily ■ Adm for tours on Sun

The most attractive aspect of this 19th-century abbey is its painted depictions of saints.

9 Abbaye de St-Roman

MAP B3 ■ Opening times vary (check www.abbaye-saint-roman.com for details) ■ Closed Mon, 25 Dec ■ Adm

This remarkable 5th-century abbey, carved into a rock face, is the only troglodyte monastery in Europe.

10 Église des Saintes-Maries-de-la-Mer

MAP A4 ■ Pl de l'Église ■ 04 90 97 80 25 ■ Open daily (call for times) ■ Adm

A 12th-century church (see p41) that has a taurobolium altar from the 4th-century BC.

Château de Beaucaire

Places to Eat

1 Une Table au Sud, Marseille

MAP C4 ▪ 2 Quai du Port ▪ 04 91 90 63 53 ▪ Closed Sun & Mon ▪ €€€

Run by a husband and wife team, this esteemed restaurant is known for its refined and creative cuisine. The restaurant offers an impressive view over Marseille's Vieux Port and the 19th-century basilica.

Interior of Une Table au Sud

2 Sauvage, Aix-en-Provence

MAP C4 ▪ 24 rue de l'Aumône Vieille ▪ 04 42 91 37 56 ▪ Closed Sat & Sun ▪ €€€

Chef Loïc Pétri offers modern menus inspired by the daily market produce.

3 La Cuisine des Anges, St-Rémy-de-Provence

MAP B3 ▪ 4 rue 8 mai 1945 ▪ 04 90 92 17 66 ▪ Closed Sun; Mon, Tue, Thu, Fri & Sat L; Feb & Mar: Mon–Thu; Jan ▪ €€

The restaurant at this B&B, Le Sommeil des Fées, is a local favourite for lamb tagine and Provençal classics.

4 Le Garage, Martigues

MAP C5 ▪ 20 av Frédéric Mistral ▪ 04 42 44 09 51 ▪ Closed Sun, Mon, Aug, 2 wks Jan ▪ €

Chef Fabien Morreale cooks refined fusion dishes in an Art Deco garage.

5 Le Mazet du Vaccarès, Arles

MAP B4 ▪ D37, rte Albaron Villeneuve ▪ 04 90 97 10 79 ▪ Closed Mon–Thu, Sun D ▪ No credit cards ▪ €€

Located on the edge of the Étang de Vaccarès, this is the place to sample Camargue clams in lemon cream. No vegetarian options.

6 Drum Café, Arles

MAP B4 ▪ Luma Arles, Parc des Ateliers, 33 av Victor Hugo ▪ 04 65 88 10 00 ▪ Closed Mon & Tue ▪ €€

Set in the Luma cultural centre, this restaurant caters to an artistic crowd. Open for lunch only.

7 L'Oustau de Baumanière, Les-Baux-de-Provence

MAP B4 ▪ CD 27 ▪ 04 90 54 33 07 ▪ Closed early Mar–mid-May & early Oct–mid-Dec: Wed & Thu ▪ €€€

Superb French cuisine made with local produce sourced from Baumanière's organic vegetable garden.

8 Les Vieilles Canailles, Aix-en-Provence

MAP C4 ▪ 7 rue Isolette ▪ 04 42 91 41 75 ▪ Closed Mon & Sun ▪ €€

Locals praise the unpretentious dishes at this laid-back bistro and wine bar.

9 El Campo, Saintes-Maries-de-la-Mer

MAP A4 ▪ 13 rue Victor Hugo ▪ 04 90 97 84 11 ▪ Closed Sun D, Mon, Feb–early Mar ▪ €€

Wash down a bull-meat casserole with a glass of Costières de Nîmes, listening to live gypsy flamenco.

10 Greenstronome, Arles

MAP B4 ▪ 7 rue des Carmes ▪ 04 90 91 07 69 ▪ Closed Mon & Tue ▪ €€€

Greenstronome's chef Jean-Luc Rabanel is famous for his accomplished plant-based menus. His more casual Greeniotage bistro is at the same address.

See map on pp80–81

🔟 The Var and Provençal Coast

Within just a 30-minute drive of the glamour of St-Tropez, you can be on a rugged mountainside so remote that you may dread nightfall. That's the charm of the Var – an intoxicating mix of the good life and an untamed landscape. In the Gorges du Verdon and Upper Var, nature is both wild and imposing; down below, on the coast, beauty assumes more rounded forms in beach resorts and casinos. Yet the Provençal tendency

Carvings, Basilica St-Maximin

to "let time take its time" unites the region. Little wonder that this is the most popular of French holiday regions.

THE VAR AND PROVENÇAL COAST

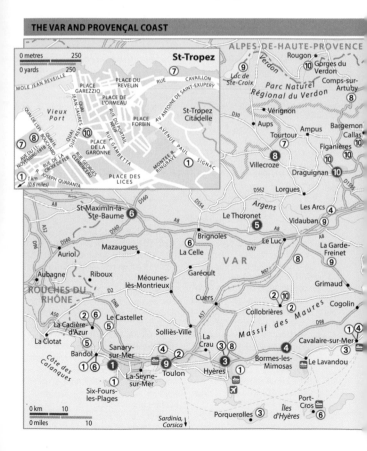

Sanary-sur-Mer harbour

1 Sanary-sur-Mer
MAP D5

The prettiest harbour in the Var remains a proper fishing port, bobbing with boats. Beyond, palm trees fringe a frontage of pastel façades. Activities range from

[Map of the Var region]

1	**Top 10 Sights**	*see pp8/–9*
1	**Places to Eat**	*see p93*
1	**Sporting and Outdoor Activities**	*see p91*
1	**Var Villages**	*see p90*
1	**Var Nightlife**	*see p92*

relaxed to intense, notably during the morning market which enlivens the Allées d'Estienne-d'Orves. Look for plaques commemorating Thomas Mann, Bertolt Brecht and other German writers who took refuge from the Nazis here in the 1930s.

2 Fréjus Old Town
MAP F5 ▪ Cathédrale St-Léonce: open 7am–7pm daily; Cloisters: Jan–Apr & Sep–Dec: 10am–1pm & 2–5pm Tue–Sun; May–Aug: 10am–6pm daily; closed 1 Jan, 1 May, 1 & 11 Nov, 25 Dec; adm (cloisters only)

Despite its relaxed image, Fréjus has an exceptional double heritage. As Forum Julii, it was the second port of the Roman Empire in the region and retains some of the oldest remains in Provence. Particularly notable are the elliptical arena and theatre *(see p42)*. Meanwhile, the town's medieval bishopric status has left it with an extraordinary group of episcopal buildings. The 13th-century Cathédrale St-Léonce *(see p47)* incorporates a wonderful octagonal baptistry from an earlier, 5th-century church, and the 14th-century cloisters have ceilings painted with bracingly lurid events from the Apocalypse.

Baptistry at Cathédrale St-Léonce

3 Villa Noailles, Hyères
MAP E6 ▪ Montée Noailles ▪ 04 98 08 01 98 ▪ Open Jan–Jun & Sep–Dec: 1–6pm Wed–Sun; Jul & Aug: 2–7pm Tue–Wed & Fri–Sun, 3–9pm Thu ▪ Closed public hols

Built for art patrons Charles and Marie-Laure de Noailles, this villa hosts changing exhibits on design, photography, fashion, and architecture.

Hilltop village of Bormes-les-Mimosas

④ Bormes-les-Mimosas
MAP E5

This is a glorious village *(see p49)*, unravelling down the hillside in a cascade of little streets, stairways, terracotta-tiled rooftops and flowers.

⑤ Abbaye du Thoronet, Le Thoronet
MAP E4 ▪ Quai Abbaye ▪ Open 10am–1pm & 2–5pm daily (Apr–Sep: to 6:30pm) ▪ Closed 1 Jan, 1 May, 1 & 11 Nov, 25 Dec ▪ Adm

This majestic 12th-century Cistercian abbey was built in a wooded dip near Lorgues. Probably the finest example of Romanesque architecture in the region, along with its sister houses, Silvacane and Sénanque *(see pp30–31)*, it rises with sober magnificence. The un-mortared stones of the church, the monks' buildings and the cloisters are decorated only by changing sunlight, their interior volumes inspiring awe and serenity. The harmony of structure and setting make contemplation unavoidable.

PERCHED VILLAGES

The Var's *villages perchés* were built as a defence against Saracen invaders who, in the 9th century, occupied parts of the Var, notably around La Garde-Freinet. Expelled in 973, they returned to wreak havoc at frequent intervals up until the 18th century. The locals therefore took to the hills for protection.

⑥ Basilica St-Maximin, St-Maximin-la-Ste-Baume
MAP D4 ▪ Open 7:30am–7:30pm daily (except during Mass)

Provence's finest example of Gothic architecture was erected to house the relics of Mary Magdalene, "discovered" on the site in 1280. The basilica appears unfinished from the outside (there is no belfry) but within, the sense of balance is stunning. So too are the treasures, notably a 16th-century altarpiece depicting the Passion of Christ, and a renowned 17th-century organ. Mary Magdalene's remains are in a reliquary and a marble sarcophagus in the crypt.

⑦ Massif de l'Esterel
MAP G4

As the rugged red rocks of the Esterel range plunge into the blue of the Mediterranean, they create creeks and contrasts of stirring beauty. Inland, the tough, volcanic mountains may rise no higher than 600 m (2,000 ft) but the landscape is of breathtaking gorges, passes and peaks. Many paths and tracks *(see p57)* provide access to the mountainscape and its rich tree life. Take the Perthus or tougher Mal Infernet valleys – in the footsteps of brigands who hid out here.

Massif de l'Esterel

8 Caves, Villecroze
MAP E4 ■ Open times vary, visit www.villecroze-tourisme.com for details (check for guided tours) ■ Adm

Riddling the wall of rock that dominates the medieval village, these caves were first home to pre-historic people and, later, provided refuge against Saracen invaders. Most startling, however, is a cave on the north side of the village, trans-formed by a 16th-century nobleman into a four-storey, fortified house, with Renaissance frontage and carved stone windows. A spring creates a cascade which waters gardens below.

Troglodyte caves at Villecroze

9 Toulon
MAP E5 ■ Musée de la Marine: pl Monsenergue; open Sep–Jun: 10am–6pm Wed–Mon, Jul–Aug: 10am–6pm daily; adm

France's biggest, and once gritty, naval port has made a remarkable comeback. Explore the spruced-up old port, take the cable car up Mont Faron for spectacular views and visit the outstanding Musée de la Marine.

10 Musée des Arts et Traditions Populaires, Draguignan
MAP F4 ■ 75 pl Georges Brassens ■ Open 9am–noon & 2–6pm Tue–Sat ■ Closed 1 Jan, 1 May, 25 Dec ■ Adm

Housed in 18th-century buildings in the old town, this is one of the best ethnographic museums in France. Its displays illustrate the story of Provençal life from its earliest days to the beginning of the 20th century.

A DAY'S DRIVE IN THE MASSIF DES MAURES

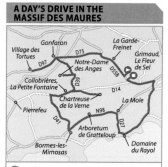

▶ MORNING

Start in the village of Grimaud and take the D558 up to **La Garde-Freinet** *(see p90)*. Continue 7 km (4 miles) before turning left (D75) through Gonfaron on the D97 to reach the Village des Tortues, where you can see the rare native Hermann tortoise *(Carnoules: open 10am–6pm Wed, Sat & Sun; Nov–mid-Mar: to 5pm; adm)*. Head back and take the D39 to **Collobrières** *(see p90)*. At Col des Fourches head up to Notre-Dame des Anges; there's a chapel and fine views.

About 3 km (2 miles) before Collobrières, turn left (D14) to the Chartreuse de la Verne, a 12th-century Carthusian monastery *(Quartier Verne: open Apr–May & Oct–Nov: 11am–5pm daily; Feb–Mar & Dec: 11am–5pm Wed–Mon; Jun–Sep: 11am–6pm daily; adm)*. Then double back to Collobrières. Stop for a drink or lunch at **La Petite Fontaine** *(see p93)*.

AFTERNOON

Leave towards Pierrefeu, but 2 km (1 mile) later turn left (D41) towards **Bormes-les-Mimosas**. The drive takes you over the Col de Babaou to the N98. Turn left towards La Mole, but stop off at the Arboretum de Gratteloup (N98), a forest garden.

Continue to La Mole, then turn right (D27) to the Col du Canadel and stop at the **Domaine du Rayol** *(see p54)* gardens. Returning to Grimaud, enjoy dinner at **Le Fleur de Sel** *(4 pl du Cros; 04 94 43 21 54; closed Wed & Thu; €€)*.

See map on pp86–7 ←

Var Villages

 Mons
MAP F4

Almost 820 m (2,700 ft) up, Mons has the heritage to match its grandiose position: remains of the great Roche Taillée Roman aqueduct run nearby. In the village itself, narrow alleys wind around ancient porches, pretty arcades and the wonderful 12th-century church.

 Collobrières
MAP E5

It's difficult to resist a village claiming to be "world capital of candied chestnuts". In the heart of the Massif des Maures (see p89), Collobrières is surrounded by forested slopes.

3 Ramatuelle
MAP F5

Although swamped by the overspill from St-Tropez in summer, Ramatuelle remains a lovely hilltop village. Its tiny streets and vaulted passages are heavy with flowers.

4 Les Arcs-sur-Argens
MAP F4

With the medieval castle up top, the rest of the old village hugs the rocky promontory. Its labyrinth of streets and vaulted stairways unfold to the modern village below.

5 Le Castellet
MAP D5

The only access to this glorious village is via two gates in its 13th-century walls. Within, steep paved streets climb tortuously to the feudal castle. Views over olive groves to the sea are outstanding.

The village of Le Castellet

 La Cadière-d'Azur
MAP D5

The medieval St-Jean gate is a great introduction to this ravishing maze of streets set above the terraced hillsides and vineyards of Bandol. The panorama is breathtaking.

 Tourtour
MAP F4

Remote, perched at 600 m (2,000 ft) up and surrounded by pine forest, Tourtour is a picturesque tangle of streams, medieval buildings and old stone streets leading to a main square lined with restaurants.

8 Comps-sur-Artuby
MAP F4

This is high, wild country, where the Knights Templar made a base. The 12th-century St-André chapel testifies to their presence, and affords unbeatable views over the nearby Artuby Gorges.

 La Garde-Freinet
MAP F5

Nestling amid forests of cork-oak and chestnut, La Garde-Freinet stands sentry to the wild Maures Mountains. Higher still are the ruins of the medieval village fortified by Saracens.

10 Callas
MAP F4

Fortified on the side of a green hill, Callas has a winding, self-contained charm imposed by its isolation near the edge of the Canjuers Plateau. It's also a fine base for walking the nearby Pennafort Gorges.

Sporting and Outdoor Activities

1 Watersports

The Var coast offers everything, from sailing and tuna-fishing to windsurfing and parascending. Resorts awarded the *"Station Voile"* symbol for excellent watersports facilities include Hyères and Bandol. Meanwhile, Brutal Beach at Six-Fours draws international windsurfers *(see p65)* and Cavalaire claims to be the French capital of jet-skiing.

Windsurfing at Cavalaire

2 Hill Walks in the Maures Mountains

The walking possibilities amid these forests, valleys and peaks *(see p89)* are magnificent. The two-hour Collobrières to Chartreuse de la Verne monastery trek is one of the best.

3 Cycling on Porquerolles

Cars are banned on the island of Porquerolles *(see p52)*, so cycling is the most rewarding way to explore it. Hire bikes from the village.

4 Mont Faron

MAP E5

Rising up 540 m (2,000 ft) behind the city of Toulon, Mont Faron is most dramatically reached by cable car from boulevard Admiral Vence. The views and walks are terrific.

5 Golf

MAP D5 ▪ Golf de Frégate, Route de Bandol, St Cyr-sur-Mer

The Var has a dozen golf courses, of which the best-known is the Golf de Frégate, set among vineyards and olive groves and overlooking the sea.

6 Snorkelling, Port-Cros

MAP F6 ▪ Port-Cros National Park: 04 94 12 82 30

Head to La Palud beach and explore the underwater guided path to discover posidonia, coral, mother-of-pearl and brightly coloured fish. It is vital that you call the national park harbourmaster's office before setting out.

7 Coastal Walk, St-Tropez

MAP F5

Far from the crowds, the path winds around creeks and beaches, offering lovely views. From Graniers beach to Cap Camarat takes 6 hours.

8 Formula One Driving

MAP E5 ▪ AGS Formule 1, ZA Circuit du Var, Gonfaron ▪ 04 94 60 97 00

Try the one-day course, open to all drivers at the Le Luc circuit. Expensive but undeniably thrilling.

9 Sailing, Lac de Ste-Croix

MAP E3

This vast artificial lake *(see p15)* offers all sorts of boating, from pedalo to dinghy. It's also an access point for canoe trips up the gorges.

Mountain biking, Gorges du Verdon

10 Mountain Biking

Tough trail cyclists are spoiled for choice in the Var. The most dramatic trips are around the Gorges du Verdon *(see pp14–15)* but Draguignan, Figanières and Fréjus also provide challenging routes.

See map on pp86–7 ←

Var Nightlife

1 Les Caves du Roy, St-Tropez

MAP F5 ■ Av du Marechal Foch ■ www.lescavesduroy.com

The Byblos Hotel's legendary club (see p60) has a suitably strict door policy: the unfashionable are generally unfortunate. If selected, you will be at the heart of Tropezien nightlife.

2 Coquetèle, Toulon

MAP E5 ■ 397 littoral Frédéric Mistral

Enjoy creative cocktails on the covered terrace of this bar in the lively Mourillon quarter. The drinks come with wonderful sea views.

3 Casino des Palmiers, Hyères

MAP E6 ■ Av Ambroise Thomas

Renovated in the 1990s, the casino has retained its belle époque style and added on a glass dome. Alongside the gaming rooms are a hotel, restaurant and nightclub.

4 La Rhumerie, Cavalaire-Sur-Mer

MAP F5 ■ Rue du Port

This lively cocktail bar, with frequent live bands and theme nights, rocks the seaside until late.

5 El Camino, St-Raphaël

MAP F5 ■ Port Santa-Lucia

Sip a rum cocktail while you salsa, mambo and merengue the night away. There are musical dinners from Thursday to Saturday, plus Sunday brunch and afternoon garden parties.

6 Casino de Bandol, Bandol

MAP D5 ■ Pl Lucien Artaud

A stylish spot in which to play the fruit machines, the tables – or the field. The complex also boasts a reputable restaurant and sleek lounge bar, both with great views.

7 VIP Room, St-Tropez

MAP F5 ■ Résidence du Nouveau Port

A Studio 54-like vibe prevails at this exclusive supper/dance club. If you're not eating, don't bother turning up before midnight, which is when the trendy set arrives.

8 L'Opéra, St-Tropez

MAP F5 ■ Residence du Port

This pillar of the resort's jet-set nightlife since 1962 serves global cuisine amid quirky artworks. It has a waterfront cabaret-restaurant with all-white decor. In the evening, enjoy performances on the central stage by flame-throwers, exotic dancers and violin players.

The sophisticated setting at L'Opéra

9 Les Moulins de Ramatuelle, Ramatuelle

MAP F5 ■ 34 chemin des Moulins

Start the evening with an apéritif and a round of pétanque amid pine and olive trees at this bar-restaurant. Follow up with a delicious Provençal dinner. Late-night DJ sets at weekends keep the party going.

10 Bar du Port, St-Tropez

MAP F5 ■ 7 quai Suffren

This high-tech bar on the port starts early (open for breakfast at 7am) and closes late (3am). Lunch and dinner are served before DJ-driven house music kicks in.

Places to Eat

PRICE CATEGORIES

For a three-course meal for one with half a bottle of wine (or equivalent meal), taxes and extra charges.

€ under €40   €€ €40–€60   €€€ over €60

1 Les Viviers du Pilon, St-Tropez

MAP F5 ▪ 2 av Général-de-Gaulle ▪ 06 52 20 15 90 ▪ Closed Nov–Mar ▪ €€

Next to a fishmonger's overlooking the Golfe, this sunny restaurant offers some of the freshest seafood on the coast: the seared tuna with homemade pesto is sublime.

2 Hostellerie Bérard, La Cadière-d'Azur

MAP D5 ▪ 6 rue Gabriel Péri ▪ 04 94 90 11 43 ▪ Closed Mon, Tue, mid-Jan–early Feb ▪ €€€

A former monastery offers distinctly non-monastic standards of luxury and innovative Provençal cuisine.

3 Café des Jardiniers, Le Rayol-Canadel

MAP F5 ▪ Le Domaine du Rayol, av Jacques Chirac ▪ 04 98 04 44 00 ▪ Closed 2 weeks Jan, D ▪ €

Enjoy a lunch of soup, omelette and salads, using fresh produce from these lovely waterside gardens just west of St-Tropez.

4 La Vague d'Or, St-Tropez

MAP F5 ▪ Cheval Blanc, plage de la Bouillabaisse ▪ 04 94 55 91 00 ▪ Closed L (except Wed), early Oct–early May ▪ €€€

Dining at this three Michelin-starred restaurant promises to be a sensory experience. Try the set menus.

5 La Brasserie, St-Raphaël

MAP F5 ▪ 6 av de Valescure ▪ 04 94 95 25 00 ▪ Closed Sun & Mon, Jan ▪ €

This hidden gem serves French cuisine on a garden terrace shaded by lemon and magnolia trees.

6 Hostellerie de l'Abbaye de La Celle, La Celle

MAP F5 ▪ 10 pl du Général-de-Gaulle ▪ 04 98 05 14 14 ▪ Closed Jan, Tue & Wed in winter ▪ €€€

Chef Nicolas Pierantoni uses produce from this inn's organic vegetable garden to create Provençal fare.

Hostellerie de l'Abbaye de La Celle

7 La Pomme de Pin, Ramatuelle

MAP F5 ▪ Rte de Tahiti ▪ 04 94 97 73 70 ▪ Closed mid-Oct–Mar ▪ €

Mouthwatering Sardinian cuisine in a convivial setting. Try the *culurgiones*, filled with fresh sheep's cheese.

8 La Colombe, Hyères

MAP E6 ▪ 663 rte de Toulon, La Bayorre ▪ 04 94 35 35 16 ▪ Closed Mon & Tue ▪ €€

Enjoy generous portions of refined Provençal cooking at this restaurant.

9 La Bastide des Magnans, Vidauban

MAP F5 ▪ 32 av du Général Galliéni ▪ 04 94 99 43 91 ▪ Closed Mon D & Wed D ▪ €€

La Bastide takes the simplest local ingredients and comes up with a balanced array of wonderful tastes.

10 La Petite Fontaine, Collobrières

MAP E5 ▪ Pl de la République ▪ 04 94 48 00 12 ▪ Closing times vary, call in advance ▪ No credit cards ▪ €

Excellent, no-frills regional cooking in a characterful village restaurant.

See map on pp86–7 ←

🔟 Nice

Nice – the very name sparkles with sunlight and glamour. In the 19th century, the European aristocracy colonized the place, drawn by the glorious Bay of Angels and the mild winter weather. Artists such as Matisse and Chagall were inspired by Nice's limpid light and left their mark here *(see pp40–41)*. Millionaires and film stars would soon follow. There is another Nice, however, rooted in Mediterranean history. For centuries part of the kingdom of Savoy, Nice voted to join France only in 1860, and retains its own dialect and traditions. It is a combination of all this that makes Nice so attractive to a new generation of creative types, who in recent years have made the city livelier than ever.

Cathédrale St-Nicolas

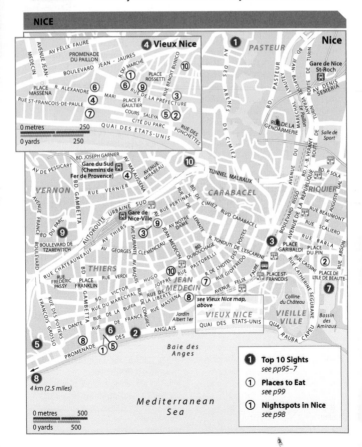

NICE

Nice

4 Vieux Nice

1 Top 10 Sights
see pp95–7

1 Places to Eat
see p99

1 Nightspots in Nice
see p98

Mediterranean Sea

Baie des Anges

4 km (2.5 miles)

0 metres 500
0 yards 500

1 Musée Matisse

MAP Q1 ■ 164 av des Arènes de Cimiez ■ Open 10am–5pm daily (to 6pm May–Oct) ■ Closed 1 Jan, Easter, 1 May, 25 Dec ■ Adm

Shortly before his death in 1954, Henri Matisse *(see p45)* donated a collection of paintings to the city he had lived in for 37 years. They have found a superb home in a 17th-century Italianate villa *(see p42)* on Cimiez Hill. Boosted by subsequent donations, the collection affords a comprehensive overview of his work, from 1890 through to the gouache cut-outs of his later years. It is made all the more effective by the display of items from his daily life.

2 Promenade des Anglais and Promenade du Paillon

MAP N5–P5, Q4–5

The promenade des Anglais owes its name to the English community that funded its construction in 1822, in order to give work to the local poor. Now flanked by traffic lanes, it sweeps majestically round the Bay of Angels, dotted with *belle époque* edifices, notably the magnificent Le Negresco hotel *(see p142)*. In contrast, the promenade du Paillon cuts a green swathe through the city to the sea and with its central waterway, it provides a tranquil alternative to walking through busy streets. It is also a venue for arts and leisure activities.

The scenic promenade du Paillon

The exterior of MAMAC

3 Musée d'Art Moderne et d'Art Contemporain (MAMAC)

MAP Q4 ■ Pl Yves Klein ■ Open 10am–6pm Tue–Sun (Nov–Apr: from 11am) ■ Closed 1 Jan, Easter, 1 May, 25 Dec ■ Adm

Conceived as a triumphal arch on four marble columns linked by transparent walkways, the museum's modern architecture is startlingly effective. The collections trace the story of the avant garde from the 1960s to the present day. Particularly notable are works by the US Pop Artists and European New Realists, including those by Nice's own Yves Klein *(see p40)*.

4 Vieux Nice

The city's heart *(see pp20–21)*, filled with the aroma and sounds of all things Niçoise and famous for its Baroque churches.

5 Musée des Beaux-Arts

MAP N5 ■ 33 av des Baumettes ■ Open 10am–6pm Tue–Sun (Nov–Apr: from 11am) ■ Closed 1 Jan, Easter, 1 May, 25 Dec ■ Adm

The 19th-century town house built for a Ukrainian princess is a marvel of Neo-Classical excess. It holds collections of art from the 17th to early 20th centuries. The first floor provides a panorama of 19th-century French art, through to the Impressionists and Post-Impressionists. On the ground floor are 17th- and 18th-century works, including sculptures by Rodin.

Opulent interior at Villa Masséna

6 Villa Masséna

MAP Q5 ▪ 65 rue de France ▪ Open 10am–6pm Wed–Mon (Nov–Apr: from 11am) ▪ Closed 1 Jan, Easter, 1 May, 25 Dec ▪ Adm

This elegant, 19th-century Italianate villa houses the Musée d'Art et d'Histoire, which has an interesting collection covering the period from Bonaparte to the 1930s. Rooms are furnished in First Empire style, and highlights include Napoleon's coronation robe and death mask.

7 Port Lympia

MAP R4

Dug in the 18th century, the port never took off commercially and remains quieter than most city harbours. It is all the more charming for that – a haven of boats and ships, surrounded by Italianate buildings.

NICE'S EXPAT COMMUNITY

Led by the British, European (notably Russian) nobility flocked to Nice in wintertime from the early 19th century. Vast, luxurious hotels, villas and places of entertainment sprung up to accommodate them. Nice became two cities – one for the wealthy and leisured northern visitors and another for working Mediterranean natives. This era disappeared with World War I, but somehow the glamour never left.

8 Parc Phoenix and Musée des Arts Asiatiques

MAP N5 ▪ 405 promenade des Anglais ▪ Park: open 9:30am–6pm daily (to 7:30pm Apr–Sep); adm ▪ Museum: open 10am–5pm Wed–Mon (to 6pm Jul–Aug); closed 1 Jan, 1 May, 25 Dec

This large floral park is a themed wonderland of world horticulture with, at its centre, Europe's biggest greenhouse. Inside the metal and glass "marquee", one wanders through recreated warm-climate zones, ranging from an equatorial forest to the Natal desert. Also present in the park is the fascinating Asian Arts Museum, a marble and glass construction that contains classical and contemporary creations from the major Asian civilizations.

Boats moored at Port Lympia

9 Cathédrale St-Nicolas

MAP N4 ■ Av Nicolas II ■ Open 10am–6pm Mon–Fri, 10am–5pm Sat, noon–6pm Sun ■ Closed during private religious events ■ Adm

The Russian community was almost as prominent in Nice as the British in the late 19th and early 20th centuries. This Russian Orthodox cathedral was completed in 1912 and fully restored in 2015.

Exterior of the regal Le Régina villa

10 Cimiez Hill and Musée National Marc Chagall

MAP Q3 ■ Av du Dr Ménard ■ Museum: open 10am–6pm Wed–Mon (to 5pm Nov–Apr) ■ Closed 1 Jan, 1 May, 25 Dec ■ Adm

When European nobility took to wintering in Nice, they colonized Cimiez Hill with magnificent villas in styles ranging from Louis XV to Neo-Gothic and Oriental. Most impressive of all is the Le Régina, where Queen Victoria once stayed. Also on Cimiez Hill is the museum which houses Chagall's 17 great works on the "Biblical Message" (see p40). The collection was supplemented by oil paintings, sketches, pastels and gouaches, donated by the artist. Chagall also created stained-glass windows, a mosaic and tapestry for the museum.

A MORNING WALK AROUND NICE

▶ Start at the **Tourist Office** (5 promenade des Anglais), then turn left along avenue de Verdun to place Masséna, the city's central square. Take in the glorious red façades, gardens and ornamental fountains before crossing to enter **Vieux Nice** (see pp20–21) on rue Alexander Mari. Turn right into rue de l'Opéra and left into rue St-François-de-Paule, an old-fashioned street with long-established shops, notably Auer for confectionery (No. 7) and Alziari for olive oil (No. 14). Proceed to **cours Saleya** (see p20) for the celebrated flower market, then turn into tiny rue St-Gaëtan to soak up the old town atmosphere. Before leaving the old town, make sure you take in the cathedral, the magnificent **Palais Lascaris** (see p20), **place St-François** (see p20) fish market and the shop-filled rue Pairolière.

Emerge into the relative peace and 18th-century harmony of place Garibaldi, then take rue du Dr-Claudo to the splendid **MAMAC** (see p95). You can't miss the adjacent Bibliothèque Louis Nucéra, designed as a gigantic human bust with a cube for a head (2002), before continuing along boulevard Carabacel with its elaborate mansions.

At place Magenta, forget culture and start shopping. For designer fashion proceed into rue Paradis then avenue de Suède; rue de Rivoli then brings you to the legendary **Le Negresco** (see p143). If you're feeling rich, lunch in its **Chantecler** restaurant (see p99); if watching the pennies, have a look anyway: its interior abounds in ornate treasures.

See map on p94 ←

Nightspots in Nice

Bar des Oiseaux
MAP Q5 ■ Corner of rue
St Vincent & rue d'Abbaye ■ Closed
Sun & Mon

Francophiles will enjoy the theme
nights – philosophy, sing-songs and
cabaret – while the rest can sip a
drink amid a lively crowd at this
colourful bar in the old town.

2 La Civette du Cours
MAP Q5 ■ 1 cours Saleya

"Bar sympa", they say in French,
which means friendly and appealing –
it's especially so for the young,
artistic and mildly eccentric.

3 La Cave Romagnan
MAP P4 ■ 22 rue d'Angleterre

One of the oldest wine bars in town,
with live music on Saturday nights
and local art on the walls.

4 Le Six
MAP Q5 ■ 6 rue Raoul Bosio

In the heart of Vieux Nice, this gay-
friendly bar has live music, go-go
dancers and karaoke every single
night in the summer.

5 Le Bar du Negresco
MAP N5 ■ 37 promenade
des Anglais

No techno here in the bar of the
palatial Le Negresco *(see p143)*.
Just a cosmopolitan ambience amid
wood panelling and deep armchairs,
which give the place the pleasingly
languorous air of a fine club.

Wayne's, a lively British-style pub

6 Wayne's
MAP Q5 ■ 15 rue de la
Préfecture

This pub in Vieux Nice is a home-
from-home for British expats and
tourists. Good beer, pub food, live
music, table dancing and a terrace.

7 Ma Nolan's
MAP Q5 ■ 2 rue St-François-
de-Paule

This is the number-one Irish pub to
go to in Nice. Pints of Guinness,
cooked dinners like grandma used to
make, televised sport and free Wi-Fi
make this a favourite hangout for
expats. (One of two locations.)

8 High Club – Studio 47
MAP N5 ■ 45 promenade
des Anglais

A popular disco with dancefloors
on two levels – the High Club for
trendy 20–30-year-olds, and Studio
47 for over-30s in search of a more
refined atmosphere.

9 Le Shapko Bar
MAP P4 ■ 5 rue Rossetti
■ 07 55 67 89 89

A popular jazz club that features
a different band every night around
9:45pm, followed by late-night jam
sessions. Reach early for a good seat.

10 Le Glam
MAP P4 ■ 6 rue Eugène
Emanuel

International DJs play techno and
house music at this LGBTQ+ dance
club, which also hosts drag shows.

Le Bar du Negresco

Places to Eat

1 Le Chantecler

MAP N5 ▪ 37 promenade des Anglais ▪ 04 93 16 64 10 ▪ Closed Mon, Tue, Wed–Sun L ▪ €€€

Le Chantecler offers a truly palatial setting within the iconic Le Negresco for Virginie Basselot's Michelin-starred Provençal-inspired haute cuisine (see p62).

Grand entrance to Le Chantecler

2 Jan

MAP R4 ▪ 12 rue Lascaris ▪ 04 97 19 32 23 ▪ Closed Sun, Mon, Tue–Sat L ▪ €€€

South African chef Jan Hendrik van der Westhuizen wows locals and visitors alike with his twist on the traditional ingredients of Provence.

3 Chez Acchiardo

MAP Q5 ▪ 38 rue Droite ▪ 04 93 85 51 16 ▪ Closed Sun ▪ No credit cards ▪ €

Locals sip their apéritifs at the counter and from the kitchen comes simple, flavoursome food, including classic *salade Niçoise*.

4 Racines Bruno Cirino

MAP P3 ▪ 3 rue Clément Roassal ▪ 04 93 76 86 17 ▪ €€

Vegetables are the highlight of the menu at celebrated chef Bruno Cirino's modern bistro. The weekday set lunch menu offers unbeatable value.

5 Le Safari

MAP Q5 ▪ 1 cours Saleya ▪ 04 93 80 18 44 ▪ €€

Seafood and meat dishes on one of the liveliest terraces of Vieux Nice.

6 La Merenda

MAP Q5 ▪ 4 rue Raoul Bosio ▪ Closed Sat, Sun, bank hols ▪ No credit cards ▪ €

Dominique le Stanc turned his back on super-chef stress to open this little restaurant. Note this reassuringly simple place has no telephone.

7 Geppetto

MAP Q4 ▪ 9 rue Chauvain ▪ 04 93 16 86 27 ▪ Closed Mon, Tue, Wed–Thu D ▪ €

Reserve or be prepared to queue for Nice's most authentic Italian cuisine, in the city's friendliest dining room.

8 Le Boccaccio

MAP Q5 ▪ 7 rue Masséna ▪ 04 93 87 71 76 ▪ €€

The decor of this seafood restaurant recalls that of a schooner – but it's stylish, rather than kitsch.

9 Alounak

MAP P4 ▪ 3 rue d'Alsace Lorraine ▪ 04 93 85 86 50 ▪ Closed Sun L ▪ €

One of the region's top vegetarian and vegan restaurants (they also serve meat and seafood dishes).

10 La Petite Loge

MAP Q4 ▪ 10 rue de la Loge ▪ 04 93 01 63 28 ▪ Closed Sun–Wed, Thu–Sat L ▪ €

Atmospheric wine bar with delicious tapas-inspired dishes that marry well with the fabulous array of wines. It's tiny, so reserve in advance.

See map on p94

≋🔟 Monaco and the Riviera

**Mosaic domed ceiling,
Villa Kérylos**

The French Riviera, running from Cannes to the Italian border, is one of the most iconic stretches of Mediterranean coastline. In the 19th century its balmy winter climate attracted plutocrats, princes and their entourages, and its clear sunlight and vivid colours drew a new breed of painters. In the 1920s it became a summer resort for the first time, and in the 1950s and 1960s it was the epitome of jet-set chic. In high summer there seems to be hardly a square metre of beach, a yacht mooring, parking space or café table left vacant. Meanwhile, the enclave of Monaco, an independent state since the 14th century, has a character and mystique all of its own.

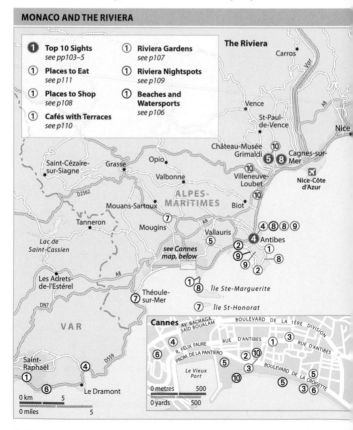

MONACO AND THE RIVIERA

① **Top 10 Sights**
see pp103–5

① **Places to Eat**
see p111

① **Places to Shop**
see p108

① **Cafés with Terraces**
see p110

① **Riviera Gardens**
see p107

① **Riviera Nightspots**
see p109

① **Beaches and Watersports**
see p106

Previous pages Moustiers-Sainte-Marie in the Gorges du Verdon

Interior of Casino de Monte Carlo

1 Casino de Monte Carlo

MAP H3 ■ Pl du Casino, Monte Carlo ■ Open 2pm–4am daily ■ www.montecarlosbm.com

Built in 1863 by Charles Garnier, this monument to belle époque splendour is also the heart of the region's famous gambling industry – well worth a look.

2 Villa Ephrussi de Rothschild, St-Jean-Cap-Ferrat

MAP H4 ■ 1 av Ephrussi de Rothschild ■ Open 10am–6pm daily (Jul–Aug: to 7pm); Nov–Feb: 2–6pm Mon–Fri, 10am–6pm Sat–Sun ■ Adm

The most palatial of all the villas built in the Riviera's plutocratic heyday was the dream of Beatrice Ephrussi de Rothschild (1864–1934), a daughter of the famous wealthy banking family. Its lavish Neo-Classical façade conceals an opulent interior of arcades surrounded by a covered courtyard hung with magnificent tapestries. Superb antiques and sketches by Fragonard also feature, while the gardens are just as sumptuous as the interior (see p54).

Exterior of the Prince's Palace

3 Prince's Palace, Monaco

MAP H4 ■ Pl du Palais ■ State Rooms and Grands Appartements: open Mar–Oct: 10am–6pm daily ■ Adm

Built on the site of a 13th-century Genoese fortress, the seat of the Grimaldi princes of Monaco is even more imposing inside than out. Highlights include superb frescoes of mythological scenes by 16th-century Genoese artists, the opulent blue-and-gold Louis XV Salon, the finely crafted woodwork of the Mazarin Salon and the gorgeous Throne Room. The Cour d'Honneur courtyard, with its geometrical pebble patterns, is a lovely setting for summer concerts. The Compagnie des Carabiniers du Prince, in full dress uniform, changes the guard daily at 11:55am.

4 Musée Picasso, Antibes

MAP G4 ■ Château Grimaldi, Vieux Port ■ Open mid-Jun–mid-Sep: 10am–6pm Tue–Sun (to 8pm Wed & Fri Jul–Aug); mid-Sep–mid-Jun: 10am–1pm, 2–6pm Tue–Sun ■ Closed 1 Jan, 1 May, 1 Nov, 25 Dec ■ Adm

A bishop's palace in the Dark Ages, this building then fell into the hands of the Grimaldi lords of Monaco, before becoming the seat of the royal governors of the region. Today, it is an art gallery. The museum houses 300 works by Spanish artist Pablo Picasso *(see p45)*, who worked here in 1946 and donated drawings, paintings and 100 ceramics. Works by other artists, including Miró, Léger, Ernst and Modigliani, are also on display *(see p43)*.

View over Roquebrune-Cap-Martin

6 Roquebrune-Cap-Martin

MAP H3 ■ Château de Roquebrune: pl W Ingram, open Oct–Apr: 10am–5pm daily (Nov–Jan: closed Fri); May–Sep: 10:30am–6:30pm daily ■ Closed public hols, Fri Nov–Jan ■ Adm ■ www.roquebrune-cap-martin.fr

The Château de Roquebrune, perched on its hilltop above Cap-Martin, is said to be the oldest feudal castle in France, built over 1,000 years ago *(see p49)*. It has been remodelled often – by the Grimaldi clan and, in the early 20th century, by a wealthy Englishman, Sir William Ingram. At sea level, a lovely coastal path leads all the way to Monaco, passing 19th-century villas in lush gardens.

Musée Picasso, Antibes

5 Château-Musée Grimaldi, Haut-de-Cagnes

MAP G4 ■ 9 pl du Château ■ Open 10am–noon (Jul & Aug: to 1pm), 2–6pm (Oct–Mar: to 5pm) Wed–Mon ■ Closed 1 Jan, 25 Dec ■ Adm

Built in 1309, this castle's battlements dominate the landscape of Haut-de-Cagnes. Within its walls is a sumptuous palace, built in 1620 by Jean Henri Grimaldi. Today it houses a clutch of museums and art collections including a museum of modern Mediterranean art, a museum dedicated to the olive tree, and a group of portraits of the 1930s *chanteuse*, Suzy Solidor.

7 Musée Oceanographique

MAP H4 ■ Ave St-Martin ■ Open 10am–6pm daily (Jan–Mar: to 5pm); Jul–Aug: 9:30am–8pm daily ■ Adm ■ www.oceano.mc

Founded by Prince Albert I in 1910, this clifftop museum features rare species of marine plants and animals, including a shark and coral lagoon.

THE GRIMALDIS OF MONACO

Monaco's Grimaldi dynasty is one of the oldest ruling families in the world. François Grimaldi, disguised as a monk, seized the castle in 1297. By 1489 France and Savoy recognized Monaco's independence. In 1612 Honore II was the first lord to take the title of prince. During the French Revolution the prince and his family were ousted, to be restored to their throne in 1814.

8 Musée Renoir, Cagnes-sur-Mer

MAP G4 ▪ 19 chemin des Collettes ▪ Open Apr–Sep: 10am–noon & 2–6pm Wed–Mon (10am–1pm Jun–Sep); Oct–Mar: 10am–noon & 2–5pm Wed–Mon ▪ Closed 1 Jan, 1 May, 25 Dec ▪ Adm

The former home of artist Auguste Renoir has been preserved as it was at the time of his death in 1919 *(see p45)*. Eleven of his paintings are on display, including *Les Grandes Baigneuses* (1892), along with some of his sculptures and works by his friends Raoul Dufy and Pierre Bonnard.

9 Salle des Mariages, Menton

MAP H3 ▪ Hôtel de Ville, 17 rue de la République ▪ Open 8:30am–noon & 2–4:30pm Mon–Fri ▪ Closed public hols ▪ Adm

Jean Cocteau decorated this room in Menton's town hall in 1957, adorning it with colourful images of a fishing couple and the story of Orpheus and Eurydice. More of his work can be seen in the two branches of the Musée Jean Cocteau *(see p43)*.

10 Villa Kérylos, Beaulieu-sur-Mer

MAP H4 ▪ Impasse Gustave Eiffel ▪ Open May & Oct: 10am–6pm daily (Jun–Sep: to 7pm); Nov–Apr: 10am–5pm ▪ Adm ▪ www.villakerylos.fr

Théodore Reinach (1860–1928) created this stunning building as a Classical Greek villa, in imitation of the palace of Delos in Greece. Copies of ancient mosaics and frescoes evoke the Greek city states.

Interior of Villa Kérylos

A MORNING TOUR OF THE ROCK

Chapelle de la Visitation

Rue Basse

Prince's Palace

Avenue Saint-Martin

Musée Oceanographique

Saint-Martin Gardens

▶ Start this walk around the historical part of Monaco where one of Europe's oldest ruling families, the Grimaldis, founded their principality. Visit the state apartments and the **Prince's Palace** *(see p103)*, taking in the lavish salons, throne room and 17th-century chapel. In one wing is the **Musée des Souvenirs Napoléoniens** *(Open Apr–Nov: 10am–6pm daily; Dec–Mar: 10:30am–5pm daily; adm)* housing over 1,000 items, including many of Napoleon Bonaparte's personal effects.

From place du Palais it is a short walk along rue Basse, one of the most picturesque streets in the old quarter, to the **Chapelle de la Visitation**, on place de la Visitation *(Open 10am–4pm Tue–Sun; adm)*. Housed in the Baroque chapel are works by artists Rubens and Zurbarán.

Leaving the chapel, turn right and double back along avenue St-Martin to discover the astonishing sea creatures in the **Musée Oceanographique**. You'll need to allow at least 90 minutes here to view the tanks of marine fauna from all over the world. Don't miss the aquarium with its fearsome sharks. Pause for an early lunch in the museum's restaurant and feast your eyes on the stunning views of the Riviera and the Esterel hills from its terrace before rounding off your visit with the 30-minute ride on the Monaco Tours tourist train. This leaves from the museum on a round trip past the port, the palace, casino and the ornamental gardens.

See map on pp102–3 ←

Beaches and Watersports

Vieux Port, St-Raphaël
MAP F5

St-Raphaël is the coast's top dive centre, with shipwrecks from World War II and a range of wall dives off the rocky coast. There are several dive outfits at the Vieux Port – a list is available from the tourist office.

2 Plage Helios, Juan-les-Pins
MAP G4 ▪ Open Apr–Sep: 9am–6pm daily ▪ Adm

This chic private beach, although it does not offer any watersports, is perfect for lazing on the soft sands.

3 Plage des Fossettes, St-Jean-Cap-Ferrat
MAP H4

Fringed by pine trees, this tranquil beach is popular with locals. Bring a snorkel: there's a variety of sea life to be spotted in the waters here.

4 Plage d'Agay
MAP G5

Watersports on this beautiful beach include waterskiing, windsurfing and parascending, as well as more relaxing boat excursions.

5 Plage de la Croisette
MAP G4 ▪ Open May–Sep: 8am–sunset daily ▪ Adm

One long beach stretches along the Cannes esplanade, sectioned off into tiny private beaches, with parasols, loungers and snack bars. Most of the beaches offer waterskiing.

Port Santa Lucia, St-Raphaël
MAP F5

You can try eight different types of watersports here, including parascending, waterskiing and windsurfing, just outside St-Raphaël.

7 Théoule-sur-Mer
MAP G4

The pretty beach at Théoule-sur-Mer, surrounded by hills, bustles in summer. Kayaks, pedalos and more equipment are available to rent.

8 Société des Régates d'Antibes
MAP G4 ▪ Quai Nord Port Vauban ▪ Open 8am–sunset daily

This yacht club, with centres in Juan-les-Pins and Antibes, offers windsurfing, dinghy and catamaran sailing and yacht charters for all levels.

9 Plage Belles-Rives, Juan-les-Pins
MAP G4 ▪ 33 bd Edouard Baudoin ▪ Open Jun–Sep: 9am–7pm daily ▪ Adm

This hotel beach offers a great range of adrenaline sports that include bungee-jumping and parascending.

10 Plage du Palais des Festivals, Cannes
MAP G4

Perhaps not the most luxurious beach in Cannes, but it is totally free and no more crowded than the paid beaches.

Plage de la Croisette

Riviera Gardens

1 Japanese Garden, Monaco

MAP H4 ■ Av Princesse Grace, Monte Carlo ■ Open 9am–5:45pm or 6:45pm daily, depending on season

This formal garden is a triumph of Zen horticulture and a striking contrast to most of the classic French gardens of the Riviera.

Villa Eilenroc Gardens

2 Villa Eilenroc Gardens, Cap d'Antibes

MAP G4 ■ Impasse de Beaumont ■ Open 10am–4pm Wed & Sat ■ Adm Apr–Sep

Charles Garnier, designer of the Monte Carlo Casino, built this villa in a park with trees from all over the world.

3 Jardin Exotique, Monaco

MAP H4 ■ 62 bd du Jardin Exotique ■ Open daily from 9am; Feb–Apr & Oct: to 6pm; May–Sep: to 7pm; Nov–Jan: to 5pm or dusk ■ Closed 19 Nov, 25 Dec ■ Adm ■ www.jardin-exotique.mc

The largest collection of succulent rock plants in the world, plus a 60-m (200-ft) deep cave with spectacular limestone formations (see p53).

4 Casino Gardens, Monaco

MAP H4 ■ Pl du Casino, Monte Carlo ■ Open 9am–sunset daily

Laid out around the casino (see p103) these are classic 19th-century gardens, with trim lawns and water features.

5 Villa Ephrussi de Rothschild

Gorgeous formal gardens and lily ponds surround the pink-and-white villa built by Beatrice Ephrussi de Rothschild (see p103).

6 Parc Fontvieille and Princess Grace Rose Garden, Monaco

MAP H4 ■ Av des Guelfes ■ Open sunrise–sunset daily

Here are palm and olive groves, plus a lake surrounded by 4,000 roses planted in memory of Princess Grace of Monaco.

7 Jardin Exotique, Èze

MAP H4 ■ Rue du Château ■ Open daily from 9am; Apr, May & Jun: to 6:30pm; Jul–Sep: to 7:30pm; Nov–Mar: to 4:30pm ■ Adm

The exotic gardens around the clifftop village offer superb sea views.

8 Jardin Botanique Val Rahmeh, Menton

MAP H3 ■ Av St-Jacques ■ Open Wed–Mon; Apr–Sep: 9:30am–12:30pm & 2–6pm; Oct–Mar: 9:30am–12:30pm & 2–5pm ■ Closed 1 May ■ Adm

Laid out by Lord Radcliffe in 1905, this garden is planted with a wide range of subtropical shrubs.

9 Jardin Botanique Thuret, Cap d'Antibes

MAP G4 ■ 62 bd du Cap ■ Open Mon–Fri; summer: 8am–6pm; winter: 8:30am–5:30pm ■ Closed public hols

Superb collection of trees and shrubs founded by Gustave Thuret in 1857.

10 Parc de Vaugrenier, Villeneuve-Loubet

MAP G4 ■ Av de Vaugrenier ■ Open Apr–Oct: 7am–8pm daily; Nov–Mar: 8am–6pm daily

Numerous rare plants can be seen in this park, which also features walking trails and a freshwater lagoon.

See map on pp102–3 →

Places to Shop

1 Rue d'Antibes, Cannes
MAP G4

For that absolutely fabulous Cannes look, head straight for rue d'Antibes and its string of designer boutiques, all breathtakingly expensive and dazzlingly ostentatious.

2 Avenue des Beaux-Arts and Allée Serge de Diaghilev, Monaco
MAP H4

With plenty of cash floating around, Monaco is a magnet for designer shops and haute couture. Try these two streets for the latest look.

3 La Croisette, Cannes
MAP G4

Cannes' famous esplanade is a great place for shopping or window-shopping, with famous labels such as Chanel (at No. 5), Saint Laurent (No. 17), Celine (No. 43), Louis Vuitton (No. 22) and Cartier (No. 57).

Produce on sale at Le Marché Forville

4 Le Marché Forville, Cannes
MAP G4

This open-air market overflows with flowers, seasonal fruit and vegetables, fresh fish and local products. It's a great place to buy Provençal delicacies to take home. Open daily except Mondays, when it becomes a flea market.

5 Vallauris
MAP G4

Vallauris's moribund pottery industry was revived when Picasso took an interest in the craft, and more than 100 local potters sell their work on its streets in summer.

6 Metropole Shopping Monte-Carlo, Monaco
MAP H4

Get the Monaco look at an affordable price at this shopping centre which houses a selection of designer shops selling prêt-à-porter clothes, shoes and accessories.

7 Galeries Lafayette, Menton
MAP H3 ▪ Rue de la République

You will find four levels of inter-national designer and brand-name clothes and accessories for men, women and children, all under one roof. There is free parking, too.

8 Cours Masséna, Antibes
MAP G4

One of the last authentic covered markets on the Riviera bustles with life every morning until noon. It is the perfect place for buying all sorts of local delicacies to take home.

9 Antiques Market, Antibes
MAP G4 ▪ Pl Audiberti, pl de Martyrs de la Résistance, pl Nationale

Rummage through stalls – selling everything from cut glass and statuary to antique porcelain, lace, embroidery and linen – in search of something small enough to carry home. Thursday and Saturdays, from 8am to noon.

10 Villeneuve-Loubet
MAP G4

Villeneuve-Loubet supports a thriving arts scene and is full of artists' and sculptors' studios where you can invest in an original work of art by a living artist.

Riviera Nightspots

 Baoli, Cannes
MAP G4 ▪ La Croisette ▪ Open from 8pm Tue–Sat (nightly Apr–Oct and during festivals) ▪ www.baolicannes.com

One of the Riviera's best venues, this cool but expensive club-restaurant attracts the likes of Bono and Naomi Campbell to its Asian-style garden of delights.

2 Casino de Monte Carlo
This is the epitome of Riviera glamour, luxury and gambling excess *(see p103)*.

Casino de Monte Carlo

3 Carlton Beach Club, Cannes
MAP G4 ▪ 58 bd de la Croisette

Enjoy refreshing cocktails and a Mediterranean menu along with 1950s-style Riviera glamour at this upscale beach club. Relax on the beach, on the central pontoon, at the bar or in the restaurant.

4 Jimmy'z, Monaco
MAP H4 ▪ Le Sporting Club, av Princess Grace ▪ 00 377 98 06 70 68 ▪ Open 11:30pm–dawn daily

Opened in 1974, Jimmy'z is still *the* place to party in Monaco, attracting the rich, famous and beautiful, and hosting top-name DJs. Of course all this glamour comes at a steep price. Make sure you dress to impress.

5 Casino Barrière Le Croisette, Cannes
MAP G4 ▪ 1 Jetée Albert Édouard/ 1 Espace Lucien Barrière ▪ Open daily to 5am in summer ▪ www.casinos barriere.com

Within walking distance of the Palais des Festivals and overlooking the busy Croisette, this casino offers one of the city's largest and most elegant gaming rooms.

6 Charly's Bar, Cannes
MAP G4 ▪ 5 rue du Suquet ▪ 06 98 92 40 41

With its stone-walled, cave-like interior, open-door policy, and DJs and dancing every night, the party crowd keeps coming back to this old favourite.

7 Blue Gin, Monaco
MAP H4 ▪ The Monte-Carlo Bay Hotel, 40 ave Princess Grace ▪ 00 377 98 06 03 60

As the name suggests, gin is the drink of choice here, with 17 different varieties on offer. Guests can admire the beautiful sea view while enjoying the drinks on the terrace.

8 Medusa, Cannes
MAP G4 ▪ Pl Franklin Roosevelt

Located on Cannes' legendary Palm Beach, this glamorous restaurant and club is known for its upscale cabaret performances and cocktails served till late.

9 Stars 'N' Bars, Monaco
MAP H4 ▪ 6 quai Antoine 1er ▪ www.starsnbars.com

One of the most popular club-restaurants in Monaco, whose transatlantic music and menu attract a young, wealthy clientele.

10 Chrystie, Cannes
MAP G4 ▪ 22 rue Macé ▪ 04 93 99 66 91 ▪ Closed Sun & Mon

A restaurant during the day and cocktail bar at night, this is a great place for brunch as well as dancing.

See map on pp102–3

Cafés with Terraces

Café de Paris, Monte Carlo

MAP H4 ▪ Pl du Casino

In front of the casino *(see p103)*, under white umbrellas and flower baskets with the Mediterranean in the background, the Café de Paris is a lovely place for an al fresco meal or a drink.

Le Majestic Barrière, Cannes

MAP G4 ▪ 10 Bd de la Croisette

Sip your drinks slowly on this deeply fashionable hotel terrace that attracts the crème de la crème of the film business during the International Film Festival. It's very pricey – a glass of bubbly here costs as much as a meal in many other spots.

③ Pavyllon, Monte Carlo

MAP H4 ▪ Hôtel Hermitage, sq Beaumarchais

This upscale restaurant in the belle époque Hôtel Hermitage has a slush Mediterranean terrace garden overlooking the port, the old town and the sparkling sea.

④ La Chèvre d'Or, Èze

MAP H4 ▪ 6 rue du Barri
▪ 04 92 10 66 66 ▪ Closed early Nov–early Mar, Mon (Mar), Mon–Wed L (Jul & Aug) ▪ €€€

It's worth staying at this gorgeous château hotel *(see p144)* just to enjoy breakfast on its clifftop

La Chèvre d'Or terrace, Èze

terrace, with breathtaking sea views. Try the great Mediterranean fare *(see p63)*.

⑤ Le Jardin du Martinez, Cannes

MAP G4 ▪ Hôtel Martinez, 73 bd de la Croisette

Grapefruit and lemon trees give this terrace café serving Mediterranean dishes the air of a Provençal village square – albeit a very chic one.

Villa Ephrussi de Rothschild, St-Jean-Cap-Ferrat

The villa's delightful tea room and terrace, overlooking beautiful gardens and with panoramic views of the bay of Villefranche, is one of the most magical and idyllic places for a light lunch or tea along the entire Riviera *(see p103)*.

⑦ Bar du Mas, Mougins

MAP G4 ▪ Le Mas Candille, bd Clément Rebuffel

Admire the Grasse countryside as you sip a chilled glass of rosé on the stone terrace of this luxury hotel. It's a more affordable option than staying here.

⑧ Plage de la Garoupe, Cap d'Antibes

MAP G4 ▪ Closed Sun pm

Walk along the eastern shore of this exclusive part of the Riviera, and you'll come to a short strip of private beaches with several cafés.

⑨ Mirazur, Menton

MAP H3 ▪ 30 av Aristide Briand

The most breathtaking views over Menton and its port are from the lofty garden terrace of the chic restaurant Mirazur, next to the oldest avocado tree in France.

⑩ Le Cactus, Èze

MAP H4 ▪ 7 la Placette

If your budget won't stretch to the Chèvre d'Or, this modest café has the same stunning views for a fraction of the price and serves delicious *crêpes*.

Places to Eat

Terrace of Maison de Bacon

1 Maison de Bacon, Cap d'Antibes
MAP G4 ▪ 664 bd de Bacon ▪ 04 93
61 50 02 ▪ Closed Mon, Tue L, Wed L,
Nov–Feb ▪ €€€

This legendary fish restaurant has
fine views over the Baie des Anges.

2 La Table du Royal, St-Jean-Cap-Ferrat
MAP H4 ▪ 3 av Jean Monnet ▪ 04 93
76 31 00 ▪ Closed mid-Nov–mid-Jan
& mid-Aug–Sep ▪ €€€

La Table du Royal offers elegant,
modern cuisine and Riviera views.

3 La Cave, Cannes
MAP G4 ▪ 9 bd de la
République ▪ 04 93 99 79 87
▪ Closed Mon & Sat L, Sun ▪ €€

La Cave has built its stellar reputation
for excellent food since 1989

4 Le Vauban, Antibes
MAP G4 ▪ 7 rue Thuret ▪ 04 93
34 33 05 ▪ Closed Mon & Tue,
1 week June ▪ €€

Le Vauban offers perfect renditions
of French and Provençal classics.

5 Pulcinella, Monte Carlo
MAP H4 ▪ 17 rue du Portier
▪ 00 377 93 30 73 61 ▪ €€

Delicious Italian food is the speciality
in this lovely restaurant. Photos of
celebrity regulars line the walls.

6 3.14 Plage, Cannes
MAP G4 ▪ 63 bd de la Croisette
▪ 04 93 94 25 43 ▪ €€

Eat in the shade of wide parasols at
this beachside restaurant overlooking
the bay, where the chefs focus on
organic and gluten-free dishes.

7 La Tonnelle, Île St-Honorat
MAP G4 ▪ 04 92 99 54 08 ▪ Closed D,
mid-Nov–mid-Dec ▪ €€€

This restaurant offers splendid views
and a fish-based lunch. Wines are
made by the resident monks.

8 Le Louis XV, Monte Carlo
MAP H4 ▪ Hôtel de Paris, pl du
Casino ▪ 00 377 98 06 88 64 ▪ Closed
Tue & Wed, Mon L, Thu L & Fri L; late
Nov–late Dec ▪ €€€

The marvellous Louis XV offers a
modern culinary experience inspired
by the French Riviera (see p62)

The terrace at Les Deux Frères

9 Les Deux Frères, Roquebrune-Cap-Martin
MAP H4 ▪ Pl des Deux Frères ▪ 04 93
28 99 00 ▪ Closed mid-Oct–mid-Nov
▪ €€€

Provençal dishes based on lamb,
duck and seafood are served in this
delightful restaurant.

10 Le Pérousin, Cagnes-sur-Mer
MAP G4 ▪ 4 rue Hippolyte Guis ▪ 09
53 55 61 92 ▪ Closed Nov ▪ €€

The intimate setting is as charming as
the seasonal cuisine, which includes
dishes cooked on an open fire.

See map on pp102–3 ←

TOP 10 Alpes-Maritimes

Technically, the Riviera is part of the Alpes-Maritimes *département*, but inland the landscape changes dramatically and the region's forested mountains, deep river gorges and medieval hilltop villages seem a million miles from the busy seaside resorts. High in the mountains is the Mercantour, a region of rocky summits and glaciers, which shelters chamois, ibex and rare lammergeier vultures. In winter, Alpes-Maritimes is one of France's favourite ski areas.

La Trophée d'Auguste at La Turbie

① La Trophée d'Auguste
MAP H3 ■ Av Albert 1er, La Turbie
■ Open Tue–Sun; mid-Sep–mid-May: 10am–1:30pm & 2:30–5pm; mid-May–mid-Sep: 9:30am–1pm & 2:30–6:30pm
■ Closed public hols ■ Adm

This remarkable Roman monument is the only one of its kind still in existence. It can be seen from afar and offers fine views along the Riviera. A museum shows a 3D film about the monument's history (see p42).

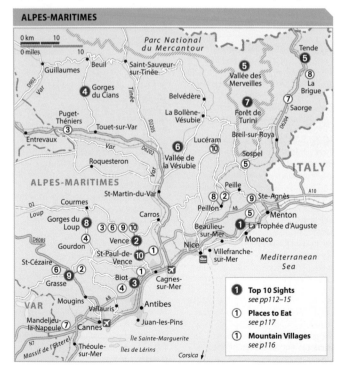

ALPES-MARITIMES

The medieval village of Vence, perched atop a crag

2 Vence
MAP G4

Vence is a gem of the region, with an unbeatable location on a high crag, and sweeping views. The medieval centre is ringed by formidable battlement walls and is entered through a massive stone gateway, to a labyrinth of cobbled streets and tall stone houses. A small cathedral, dating from the 11th century and built on the site of a Roman temple, stands on place Clemenceau.

3 Biot
MAP G4 ■ Musée Fernand Léger: Chemin du Val-de-Pôme; open 10am–5pm Wed–Mon (to 6pm May–Oct); closed 1 Jan, 1 May, 25 Dec; adm; www.musees-nationaux-alpesmaritimes.fr/fleger ■ La Verrerie de Biot: Chemin des Combes; open 10am–1pm & 2–6pm Mon–Sat, 10:30am–1:30pm & 2:30–6pm Sun & public hols; adm; www.verreriebiot.com ■ www.biot.fr

The pretty little town of Biot sits on a hilltop among pinewoods. It is renowned for its high-quality decorative glassware, which you can watch being blown at La Verrerie de Biot. The wonderful Musée Fernand Léger, also in the village, contains more than 400 drawings and paintings by the artist *(see p44)*.

4 Gorges du Cians
MAP G3

The deep gorge carved through the mountains by the River Cians is made all the more spectacular by the deep red of the exposed rock. The river descends 1,600 m (5,250 ft) in just 25 km (15 miles) between the hilltop villages of Beuil and Touet-sur-Var, where the Cians meets the larger river Var. The canyon *(see p50)* is at its narrowest and most spectacular at Pra d'Astier, which is about midway between the two villages.

Red rocks of Gorges du Cians

5 Vallée des Merveilles and Musée des Merveilles

MAP H2 ■ Musée des Merveilles: av du 16 Septembre 1947, Tende; open 10am–6pm Wed–Mon (to 5pm mid-Sep–mid-Jun); closed 1 Jan, 1 May, 2 wks mid-Nov, 25 Dec

High in the Parc National du Mercantour (see p50), this valley shelters a treasury of Bronze Age art (see p36). Rock carvings dating from 1800–1500 BC are scattered over the slopes of the 2,870-m (9,400-ft) Mont Bégo. They are almost impossible to find without a guide, but the Musée des Merveilles has many examples.

Petroglyphs, Vallée des Merveilles

6 Vallée de la Vésubie

MAP H3 ■ www.vesubian.com

Two streams merge at St-Martin-Vésubie to form the River Vésubie, which flows through landscapes of pinewoods, meadows, forested peaks and narrow canyons to join the Var 24 km (15 miles) north of Nice. The valley is dotted with attractive

Pointe des Trois Communes

SKIING IN THE ALPES D'AZUR

High above the balmy coast, the slopes and summits of the Alpes d'Azur (above) are deeply covered in snow in winter, with excellent skiing conditions, and there are more than 250 pistes, ranging from black to green runs, in well-equipped resorts. The best known is Isola 2000, with three black runs, 13 red, 22 blue and seven green.

villages, and the river is at its most scenic where it passes through the Gorges de la Vésubie, a canyon of coloured rock walls.

7 Forêt de Turini

MAP H3

A moist micro-climate, created by warm sea air rising over the cooler mountains, waters this mountain forest, where thick beech, maple and chestnut woods cloak the lower slopes, and huge pines rise on the higher mountainsides. From Pointe des Trois Communes, on the fringe of the forest at an altitude of 2,082 m (6,830 ft), there is a panorama of the Alpine foothills and the Parc National du Mercantour (see p50).

8 Gorges du Loup
MAP G3

In this most spectacular of the region's river canyons *(see p51)*, the River Loup has sliced its way deep into the rock to create a series of waterfalls. These include Cascade de Courmes, rapids and deep potholes, such as the Saut du Loup.

9 Grasse
MAP G4 ■ Musée Internationale de la Parfumerie: 2 bd du Jeu de Ballon; open 10am–5:30pm daily (May–Sep: to 7pm); closed 1 Jan, 1 May, 25 Dec; adm; Musée du Parfum: 20 bd Fragonard; open 9am–6:30pm daily

Grasse's air is scented by the perfume factories for which it has been famous for over four centuries. Vast quantities of blooms are processed here for their essential oils, and a spectacular jasmine festival is held each August. You can buy perfumes at the Musée Internationale de la Parfumerie. The Musée du Parfum in the Fragonard factory traces the history of perfume, with displays of rare perfumery objects such as medieval pomanders.

The diminutive Fondation Maeght

10 Fondation Maeght, St-Paul-de-Vence

One of the finest small modern art museums in the world, the Maeght *(see p33)* includes work by Marc Chagall, Joan Miró, Fernand Léger, Alexander Calder, Alberto Giacometti, and many more 20th-century artists. The only permanent displays are the large sculptures in the grounds.

A WALK THROUGH MEDIEVAL VENCE

A giant ash tree, Le Frêne (The Ash) is your landmark for the beginning of this two-hour stroll through the old quarter of Vence *(see p113)*, with its stone-paved streets and medieval houses, which huddle inside a ring of 13th-century battlements. Before entering the walls through the 16th-century Porte du Peyra, visit the Château de Villeneuve, which hosts a changing programme of modern art and design exhibitions.

After walking through the gateway, turn right, and allow half an hour to walk along the rue du Marché, where rows of shops selling herbs, fruit, fresh pasta and fish will make your mouth water. At the end of the rue du Marché, turn left and walk across place Surian and place Clemenceau to the Cathédrale Notre-Dame de la Nativité – look out for Roman inscriptions dating back almost 2,000 years on the masonry of the buildings either side of it, carved when Vence was the Roman settlement of Vintium. Also look for the oak choir stalls carved with satirical figures, commissioned by a witty 17th-century bishop.

Leave the square by its north side, through the arched passage Cahours, then walk up rue du Séminaire and turn left to follow the old walls along rue de la Coste. Leave the old quarter by the Portail Levis, which takes you back on to place du Frêne. There are several cafés and restaurants here, such as **Auberge des Seigneurs** *(see p117)* where you can enjoy a drink and snack.

See map on p112

Mountain Villages

 St-Paul-de-Vence
The prettiest and best known of the region's *villages perchés* (see p88), St-Paul (see pp32–3) was first built as a refuge from Saracen raiders. From its ramparts there are terrific views down to the sea.

Beautiful St-Paul-de-Vence

 Peillon
MAP H3
Peillon's red-tiled houses seem to grow out of the hilltop itself, rising in tiers to a cobbled square with great views of the forested valley. It seems barely changed since the Middle Ages.

 Puget-Théniers
MAP G3
The village of Puget-Théniers stands where the Roudoule river meets the Var, overlooked by the ruins of the Château-Musée Grimaldi (see p104). The 13th-century Knights Templar church has a beautiful 16th-century altarpiece (see p47).

 Gourdon
MAP G4
From the village square, where the hillside drops into a limestone gorge, you can see all the way down the Loup valley to the coast.

5 **Sospel**
MAP H3
Colourful arcaded houses and a Baroque church are features of this pretty mountain village near the Italian border. Badly damaged in World War II, it has now been lovingly restored.

 St-Cézaire-sur-Siagne
MAP F4 ■ Grotte de St-Cézaire: rte de Grasse; open 10am–noon, 2–5pm (Jun-Aug: to 6pm); closed mid-Nov–Jan; adm
This hill village has been inhabited since the Roman era and has medieval walls and watch towers. Nearby are the grottoes of St-Cézaire, an underground wonderland.

 Saorge
MAP H3
The clifftop location rivals Gourdon's for dizzying effect, and the village is a little-changed crescent of 15th- to 17th-century pastel houses. It has two pretty churches, and splendid views.

8 **La Brigue**
MAP H2
Unspoiled La Brigue has cobbled streets, arcaded buildings and the church of Notre-Dame-des-Fontaines, with its superb medieval frescoes.

 Ste-Agnès
MAP H3
At 671 m (2,200 ft), Ste-Agnès is the highest of the coastal *villages perchés*. There are some great walking trails nearby, in the Gorbio valley.

10 **Lucéram**
MAP H3
Here, tall old houses are set around a 17th-century Rococo church and an onion-domed clock tower.

Medieval village of Lucéram

Places to Eat

PRICE CATEGORIES

For a three-course meal for one with half a bottle of wine (or equivalent meal), taxes and extra charges.

€ under €40   €€ €40–€60   €€€ over €60

① Les Terraillers, Biot
MAP G4 ▪ 11 Chemin Neuf ▪ 04 93 65 01 59 ▪ Closed Mon, Tue, mid-Oct–Nov ▪ €€€

This sophisticated restaurant is set in a 16th-century pottery mill. The dishes are rich and flavourful and the wine list superb.

② La Bastide St-Antoine, Grasse
MAP G4 ▪ 48 av Henri Dunant ▪ 04 93 70 94 94 ▪ Closed last week Feb ▪ €€€

With a Michelin star, this fine restaurant serves regional dishes on the garden terrace of a charming 17th-century Provençal house.

③ L'Ambroisie, Vence
MAP G4 ▪ 37 av Alphonse Toreille ▪ 04 93 58 78 58 ▪ Closed Mon L, Tue, Wed ▪ €€

Chef Bruno Seillery serves refined Provençal cuisine in this delightfully updated former 17th-century chapel.

④ Les Arcades, Biot
MAP G4 ▪ 14/16 pl des Arcades ▪ 04 93 65 01 04 ▪ Closed Mon (& Sun D in winter) ▪ €€

Run by three generations of the same family, this unpretentious inn, decorated with colourful works of art, is popular with locals for its fixed-price menus of traditional dishes such as pistou soup.

⑤ Hostellerie Jérôme, La Turbie
MAP H3 ▪ 20 rue du Comté de Cessole ▪ 04 92 41 51 51 ▪ Closed L, Sun, Mon, Dec–mid-Feb ▪ €€€

Only open in the evenings, this fine restaurant serves inventive dishes such as scampi in a *verveine* crust.

⑥ Auberge des Seigneurs, Vence
MAP G4 ▪ 1 pl du Frêne ▪ 04 93 58 04 24 ▪ Closed Sun, Mon, mid-Dec–mid-Jan ▪ €

Spit-roasted local lamb and chicken are among the mouth-watering choices at this friendly medieval inn complete with an open fire.

⑦ L'Oasis, La Napoule
MAP G4 ▪ 6 rue Jean-Honoré Carle ▪ 04 93 49 95 52 ▪ Closed mid-Dec–end Jan, Sun–Tue, Wed–Fri L ▪ €€€ (bistro €€)

A Riviera institution, L'Oasis offers a unique menu in a beautiful setting, plus a deli, bakery and wine cellar.

Delicious dessert at L'Oasis

⑧ Auberge de la Madone, Peillon
MAP H3 ▪ 3 pl Auguste Arnulf ▪ 04 93 07 91 17 ▪ Closed Wed, mid-Nov–Jan ▪ €€€

Enjoy classic Provençal cuisine on this restaurant's terrace overlooking a medieval village.

⑨ Les Lavandes, Vence
MAP G4 ▪ 8 rue du Marché ▪ 04 93 32 61 52 ▪ Closed Thu ▪ €€

The husband-and-wife team here serve delicious Franco-Thai cuisine.

⑩ La Farigoule, Vence
MAP G4 ▪ 15 av Henri Isnard ▪ 04 93 58 01 27 ▪ Closed Mon, Tue, late Nov–Christmas ▪ €€

Classic Provençal cuisine attracts regulars to this cosy spot.

See map on p112

TOP 10 Alpes-de-Haute-Provence

Stained glass at Moustiers

One of the highest and wildest parts of France, and indeed Europe, Alpes-de-Haute-Provence presents a sharp contrast to the foothills and valleys of the Var to the south and the rolling Vaucluse to the west. Summers are hot, winters are bitterly cold, and life in these harsh mountains is hard – which is why so much of Haute-Provence is sparsely inhabited. The Durance river flows through the region to meet the Rhône north of Aix, and tributaries such as the Verdon cut spectacular gorges through the limestone rock of the mountains, adding to the breathtaking views, cool clear air and pockets of wilderness typical of this beautiful region. The area also offers a range of sports from whitewater canoeing, to hang-gliding, to high-country walking.

ALPES-DE-HAUTE-PROVENCE

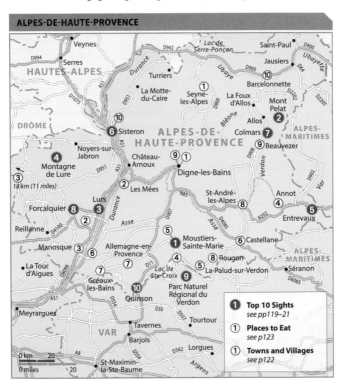

①	**Top 10 Sights** see pp119–21
①	**Places to Eat** see p123
①	**Towns and Villages** see p122

Aerial view over Moustiers-Sainte-Marie

1 Moustiers-Sainte-Marie
MAP E3 ▪ Musée de la Faïence: rue du Seigneur de la Clue; open Apr–Oct: 10am–12:30pm, 2–6pm Wed–Mon (Jul & Aug: to 7pm); Nov–Mar: 10am–12:30pm, 2–5pm Sat, Sun & school hols; closed Jan; adm

Moustiers, loud with the sound of a swift-running stream which flows through the middle of the village, is simply delightful, with its tall old houses, plane trees and, for those who can face the climb, a superb view of the Gorges du Verdon from the clifftop church of Notre-Dame-de-Beauvoir *(see p48)*. The village is famed for its faïence ware, and you can see wonderful examples in the Musée de la Faïence *(see p48)*.

2 Mont Pelat
MAP F2

The highest peak in the Provençal Alps rises to a height of 3,050 m (10,020 ft) and dominates a lofty landscape of bare rocky summits, marked by snow until early summer, pine forests and alpine meadows. The massif is crossed by breath-taking passes, including the Cime de la Bonette, by which the D64 road traverses the shoulder of Mont Pelat at a dizzy height of 2,860 m (9,400 ft), making it the highest pass in Europe.

3 Lurs
MAP D3

Founded before the reign of Charlemagne, during the Dark Ages, the town of Lurs was fortified as early as the 9th century AD, when it was ruled by the bishops of Sisteron and the princes of Lurs. Deserted in the 19th century, it has now become an artists' colony. There are stupendous views from the Promenade des Evêques (Bishops' Walk) leading to the chapel of Notre-Dame-de-Vie, especially colourful in spring when the wildflowers bloom.

4 Montagne de Lure
MAP D2

Deep in the heart of the Luberon, the Lure mountain – an extension of the savage massif of Mont Ventoux in neighbouring Vaucluse *(see p125)* – is Provence at its wildest, least hospitable and, some would say, its loveliest. Abandoned hamlets are reminders of Provence in the first half of the 20th century, when many rural people gave up trying to scrape a living from this harsh countryside.

5 Ville Forte, Entrevaux
MAP F3

The citadel of Entrevaux is one of the most dramatic of all the region's many fortresses. Perched on a pinnacle above this fairytale town, it can be reached only by a steep, zigzag path which passes through more than a dozen arched gateways. Lying beneath it, the impregnable Ville Forte is ringed by towers and ramparts and reached by a drawbridge over the river Var.

A tower in the Ville Forte, Entrevaux

Citadelle de Sisteron, over the Durance

6 Citadelle de Sisteron

MAP E2 ▪ 1 allée de Verdun
▪ Opening times vary, check website
▪ Adm ▪ www.citadelledesisteron.fr

Squatting on a steep-sided crag, high above the narrow valley of the River Durance, the formidable defences of the Citadelle guard one of the strategic gateways to Provence *(see p48)*. Built in the 13th century, the bastions and ramparts, crowned by towers and a chapel, are a great piece of military engineering. In the summer, they become the venue for the Nuits de la Citadelle, a festival of music, theatre and dance.

7 Fort de Savoie, Colmars-les-Alpes

MAP F2 ▪ 04 92 83 41 92 ▪ Open Jun & Sep: 10am–noon Wed, Sat & Sun, 2–5:30pm Tue, Fri; Jul–Aug: 10am–noon & 2–6pm daily; other times by appt only ▪ Adm

Perched atop medieval walls, this 17th-century fortress has a grim, businesslike look when compared

Fort de Savoie, Colmars-les-Alpes

> **NAPOLEON AT SISTERON**
>
> On 1 March 1815 Napoleon Bonaparte escaped from exile on Elba and landed at Golfe Juan. Had the citadel at Sisteron been garrisoned by Royalist troops, his attempt to regain his Imperial throne might have been foiled, but he entered the town unopposed on 5 March to begin a triumphal progress to Paris, only to meet his final defeat at Waterloo.

with the fairytale medieval castles found elsewhere in Provence. It was built to withstand cannon fire, not just arrows and siege towers. The work of master military engineer Vauban, it is a testimony to his skill. The Fort de France, the second of this former frontier garrison's strongholds, has fared less well and lies in ruins.

8 Forcalquier

MAP D3 ▪ Couvent des Cordeliers: bd des Martyrs; open 10am–1pm & 3–6:30pm daily; adm

This beguiling old town was once the seat of powerful local lords and the capital of the region. One gate of the old walled town, the Porte des Cordeliers, still survives, along with the restored cloisters and stark library of the 13th-century Couvent des Cordeliers, with its tombs of the town's medieval *seigneurs*. The convent is home to the Artemisia Museum, which celebrates the region's aromatic and medicinal plants.

⑨ Parc Naturel Régional du Verdon

MAP E3, F3

Along the river Verdon, this regional park is a huge patchwork of landscapes, ranging from the neatly cultivated lavender fields of the sunlit Valensole plateau to the forested hills and pastures of the Artuby, the awesome chasms of the Gorges du Verdon *(see pp14–15)* and the beginnings of the Alps. There are brilliant blue lakes created where the Verdon has been dammed. This is a paradise for hikers, with a network of 700 km (450 miles) of paths, bridleways and ancient mule highways.

Lavender fields of the Valensole plateau

⑩ Musée de Préhistoire des Gorges du Verdon

MAP E3 ■ Rte de Montmeyan, 04500 Quinson ■ 04 92 74 09 59 for cave tours ■ Museum: open Feb–Mar & Oct–mid-Dec: 10am–6pm Wed–Mon (to 7pm Apr–Jun, Sep); Jul, Aug: 10am–8pm daily; closed mid-Dec–Jan; adm

This museum, in a building designed by British architect Norman Foster, traces the geological, cultural and environmental evolution of human life in the Verdon and throughout Europe, with a fascinating series of displays and interactive exhibits. Guided tours visit caves where relics of early humans have been found.

A MORNING DRIVE THROUGH THE CANYON

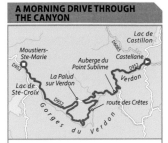

▶ Start after breakfast from the unassuming little market town of **Castellane** *(see p122)*, gateway to the canyons, and drive west on D952. The landscape becomes progressively more awe-inspiring as you enter the gorges and wind your way through towering walls of rock to **Point Sublime** *(see p14)*. This is one of the most impressive viewpoints on the tour; savour it while enjoying a coffee or a cold drink at the pleasant **Auberge du Point Sublime** *(see p123)*.

From here, drive for about 15 minutes and turn left on to the vertiginous route des Crêtes, which winds past a series of ever higher viewpoints. Don't rush this part of the drive, but stop at each viewpoint for five or ten minutes, as the views vary all the time and each one is special. Finally, the road swings around the shoulder of the massif, and far below you is the Verdon and the plateau country around the little village of **La Palud-sur-Verdon** *(see p122)*. It will take you another 30 minutes to get there, so relax when you do with another coffee at one of the village cafés.

When you are ready to set off again from La Palud, you'll find it a less daunting drive until the gorgeous turquoise waters of the **Lac de Ste-Croix** *(see p15)* come into sight. The road runs high above the lake, bringing you to the delightfully pretty village of **Moustiers-Ste-Marie** *(see p119)*. Reward yourself with lunch here, since the village happens to have two of the region's best restaurants, **La Treille Muscate** and **Ferme Ste-Cécile** *(see p123)*.

See map on p118 ←

Towns and Villages

The beautiful mountain town of Seyne-les-Alpes

 Seyne-les-Alpes
MAP E2

Military and religious buildings are scattered through this quiet mountain town: a 15th-century gate, a medieval church and a ruined citadel are the main points of interest.

 Les Mées
MAP E3

The little village of Les Mées is known for the strange rock formations called the Pénitents des Mées (see p47). Legend says these pinnacles were monks who broke their vows of chastity and were turned to stone by St Donat.

3 Simiane-la-Rotonde
MAP D3

The enigmatic Rotonde, a Roman relic, whose purpose is still a puzzle, crowns the village to which it lends its name, a picturesque cluster of old houses and churches, as well as a ramshackle medieval fort.

 Annot
MAP F3

Annot stands in unspoilt countryside in the Vaïre valley. Many houses are built into the giant sandstone glacial boulders, known as the *grès d'Annot* – some have 17th- and 18th-century carved façades.

 La Palud-sur-Verdon
MAP E3

La Palud stands on the north side of the Gorges du Verdon (see pp14–15), making it a very popular base for exploring the region.

6 Castellane
MAP F3

Castellane is a lively market town surrounded by steep mountains (see p15). The Verdon flows through it, and it is a centre for adventure sports.

 Allemagne-en-Provence
MAP E3

Allemagne-en-Provence lies between the rugged canyon country of the Verdon and the lavender fields of the Valensole plateau. It is dominated by the splendidly palatial 12th-century Château d'Allemagne.

8 St-André-les-Alpes
MAP F3

This little village bustles in summer. Built where the Verdon and Issole rivers flow into the man-made Lac de Castillon, it is a popular watersports centre, with dinghies, windsurfers and canoes for hire.

9 Beauvezer
MAP F2

Beauvezer, in the dramatic Vallée du Haut Verdon, stands 1,179 m (3,600 ft) above sea level. It enjoys a pristine natural setting, near two major ski resorts (Le Seignus and La Foux).

10 Barcelonnette
MAP F2

Provence's northernmost town is in the rugged Ubaye valley. As a result of 19th-century immigration, its architecture and festivals have a Mexican flavour. Rooftops may see a dusting of snow as late as June.

Places to Eat

 Le Grand Paris, Digne
MAP E2 ■ Hôtel du Grand Paris, 19 bd Thiers ■ 04 92 31 11 15 ■ Closed L Tue–Wed, Dec–Mar ■ €€€

This restaurant at Digne's best hotel serves classic dishes with a twist.

PRICE CATEGORIES
For a three-course meal for one with half a bottle of wine (or equivalent meal), taxes and extra charges.

€ under €40   €€ €40–€60   €€€ over €60

2 L'Auberge du Bois, Niozelles
MAP D3 ■ 191 rte de Niozelles ■ 04 92 76 61 56 ■ Closed Oct–Mar ■ €€

This unpretentious inn in the village of Niozelles serves delicious Mediterranean dishes. Tables on the terrace are set around a small fountain and shaded by pine trees.

3 Sens et Saveurs, Manosque
MAP D3 ■ 43 bd des Tilleuls ■ 04 92 75 00 00 ■ Closed Mon, Thu & Sun D ■ €€€

Superb, creative cuisine is presented in the elegantly decorated vaulted hall of a former monastery.

Elegant interior at Sens et Saveurs

4 La Treille Muscate, Moustiers-Ste-Marie
MAP E3 ■ Pl de l'Église ■ 04 92 74 64 31 ■ Closed Wed Dec–Jan ■ €€

Dine on classic dishes in a quaint restaurant by a mountain stream.

5 Ferme Ste-Cécile, Moustiers-Ste-Marie
MAP E3 ■ Rte des Gorges du Verdon ■ 04 92 74 64 18 ■ €€

Catherine and Patrick Crespin serve superb contemporary food in an 18th-century farmhouse just outside the centre.

6 Le Jardin de Célina, Valensole
MAP E3 ■ Ancien chemin d'Allemagne ■ 06 71 76 54 01 ■ Closed Wed, Mon–Thu L ■ €€

In the serene setting of the Parc Naturel Régional du Verdon, this restaurant offers modern dishes featuring Valensole produce such as truffles and almonds.

7 La Caverne, Gréoux-les-Bains
MAP E3 ■ 15 rue Grande ■ 04 92 78 19 54 ■ Closed Mon, Tue ■ €€

La Caverne may be small, but it is one of the best places in town for superb seafood and succulent Sisteron lamb.

8 Auberge du Point Sublime, Rougon
MAP E3 ■ Point Sublime ■ 04 92 83 60 35 ■ Closed mid-Oct–Apr ■ €

The location alone would make this inn special, with a terrace gazing out at the peaks of the Canyon du Verdon, but the food is also sublime, using local produce in traditional dishes.

9 L'Olivier, Dignes-les-Bains
MAP E2 ■ 1 rue des Monges ■ 04 92 31 47 41 ■ Closed Mon, Tue, Wed L, Sat L, Sun D ■ €

This lovely little restaurant with a terrace offers great value for money. Traditional French cooking with a touch of originality.

10 Le Tivoli, Sisteron
MAP E2 ■ 21 pl Réné Cassin ■ 04 92 62 26 68 ■ Closed Wed, Thu L ■ €€

The top-notch meat and fish dishes served at this small restaurant have made it a must-go-place in town.

See map on p118

TOP10 Vaucluse

At the northern gates of Provence, the Vaucluse exudes a cultured air. Its rich past – Roman heritage in Orange, papal legacy in Avignon – is reflected in summer festivals in both towns, while the perched villages of the Luberon seem purpose-built for holiday homes. But the villages are not perched on a whim and Avignon's ramparts were not for show – defence was the motive for both. In the mountains and remote parts of the Luberon, you're in Provence at its most elemental.

Lavender fields of the Abbaye Notre-Dame de Sénanque

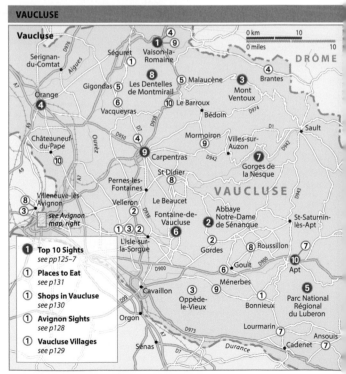

VAUCLUSE

Vaucluse

DRÔME

Serignan-du-Comtat
Séguret ① Vaison-la-Romaine ①④⑨
Gigondas ⑤ Les Dentelles de Montmirail
Orange ④
Malaucène ⑤
Brantes ④
Mont Ventoux ③
Vacqueyras ⑥ ⑩ Le Barroux
Bédoin
Sault
Châteauneuf-du-Pape ⑩
Mormoiron
Villes-sur-Auzon ⑨
④
Villeneuve-lès-Avignon ⑧③
Carpentras ⑨
St Didier ⑧
Gorges de la Nesque ⑦
Pernes-les-Fontaines
Velleron ②
VAUCLUSE
see Avignon map, right
Le Beaucet
Fontaine-de-Vaucluse ②
Abbaye Notre-Dame de Sénanque ②
St-Saturnin-lès-Apt
①③② L'Isle-sur-la-Sorgue ⑥
Gordes ②
Roussillon ⑧ ⑦
Goult ⑥
D900
Apt ⑩ ⑦
Cavaillon
Ménerbes
Oppède-le-Vieux ③
Bonnieux ①
Parc National Régional du Luberon ⑤
Orgon
Lourmarin ⑦
Ansouis
Sénas
Durance
Cadenet ⑦

① **Top 10 Sights**
see pp125–7

① **Places to Eat**
see p131

① **Shops in Vaucluse**
see p130

① **Avignon Sights**
see p128

① **Vaucluse Villages**
see p129

1 Vaison-la-Romaine

One of the finest Roman towns (see pp28–9) in Provence.

2 Abbaye Notre-Dame de Sénanque

When the lavender flowers in summer, this medieval abbey (see pp30–31) surrounded by purple fields is a spectacular sight.

3 Mont Ventoux
MAP C2

The bald-headed "Giant of Provence" is the Vaucluse's greatest landmark; one that has inspired poets, mystics and botanists for centuries. Rising 1,900 m (6,300 ft), it commands the surrounding landscape, affording astonishing views to the sea, the Alps and the Rhône. Snowcapped in winter, the summit is revealed as arid chalk in summer and buffeted

The peak of Mont Ventoux

by strong winds all year round. The lower slopes are dense with trees, 1,000 plant varieties and wildlife.

4 Théâtre Antique d'Orange
MAP B2 ■ Rue Madeline Roch ■ Open daily; Apr–Sep: 9am–6pm (to 7pm Jun–Aug); Oct–Mar: 9:30am–4:30pm (to 5:30pm Mar, Oct) ■ Adm

The finest Roman theatre (see p38) in Europe has its original stage wall, ensuring perfect acoustics.

5 Parc Naturel Régional du Luberon
MAP C3 ■ Maison du Parc, 60 pl Jean-Jaurès, Apt ■ Open 8:30am–noon, 1:30–6pm Mon–Fri (also Sat am, Easter–Sep)

The Luberon has an untamed beauty. Covering 1,500 sq km (600 sq miles), it takes in the Petit Luberon of crags, gorges and perched villages to the west and the more rounded Grand Luberon to the east. The park's headquarters (see p50) have information on walks, the ecology and the area's traditions.

Roussillon cliffs in the Luberon

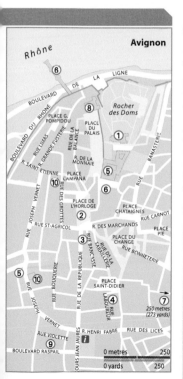

Avignon

Rhône

6 Fontaine-de-Vaucluse

MAP C3 ▪ Pétrarch Library Museum: Rive gauche de la Sorgue; open Apr–Sep: Thu–Mon; adm ▪ Musée d'Histoire Jean Garcin: 1939–45: Chemin de la Fontaine; open Apr–Sep: Thu–Mon; adm ▪ Le Monde Souterrain: Chemin de la Fontaine; open mid-Feb–mid-Nov: daily; adm

From the base of grandiose, 230-m-(750-ft-) high cliffs, Europe's most powerful spring pumps out the water which creates the River Sorgue, and attracts millions of visitors each year, as it once attracted the 14th-century Italian poet Petrarch (see p49). Downstream, the village celebrates its most famous inhabitant with a museum in one of the houses he is said to have lived in. It also has two other excellent museums; one on World War II and the other on speleology.

The Sorgue at Fontaine-de-Vaucluse

7 Gorges de la Nesque

MAP C3

The Gorges de la Nesque run for 20 km (12 miles) between the villages of Villes-sur-Auzon and Monieux. The rocky drop descends more than 300 m (1,000 ft), its sides bare or covered in scrub. Cut into the cliff, the winding road is definitely not for vertigo sufferers. The Castelleras viewpoint looks onto the Rocher du Cire (Wax Rock – so-called because of a local legend claiming that it is home to millions of bees). This is also the start of a testing walk to the bottom of the gorges, where Chapelle St-Michel is dug into the rock.

The imposing Dentelles de Montmirail

8 Les Dentelles de Montmirail

MAP C2

Probably the prettiest mountain range in Provence, the Dentelles are formed by three ridges of chalk topped by ragged crests. The French think of these as lacework (dentelles), but they can look more like fangs in rough weather. Within the range, tiny villages (Suzette, La Roque Alric) cling to the crags as if by magic and climbers are attracted to the sheer rock faces. The walking, too, is spectacularly good, notably up to St Amand, at 730 m (2,400 ft), the highest point. Round the western edge cluster the picturesque wine villages of Beaumes-de-Venise, Gigondas, Vacqueyras and Séguret. There are marked wine routes through this picturesque vineyard region (see pp64–5), and plenty of opportunities for tastings en route, but be sure to decide on a designated driver before you set off.

THE VAUDOIS MASSACRE

The bloodiest tale in Provençal history took place in Vaucluse in 1545, when Catholic Royal authorities determined to exterminate early Protestant settlers, the Vaudois. Within weeks, as many as 3,000 were dead: women and children were burned alive and villages were destroyed. The memories, and ruins, still haunt the remoter mountainsides.

9 Synagogue, Carpentras
MAP C3 ▪ Pl Maurice Charretier
▪ Open Mon–Fri for pre-booked
guided tours only; call 04 90 63 39
97 to book ▪ Closed during religious
services ▪ Adm

Expelled from France in the 14th
century, the Jews sought refuge in
parts of Provence then belonging to
the pope. This included Carpentras,
whose synagogue, founded in
1367, is the oldest still functioning
on French soil. Rebuilt in the
18th century, the synagogue looks
like neighbouring buildings from the
outside: laws forbade decoration.
Within, a monumental staircase leads
to the sumptuous two-storey area of
worship (men upstairs, women below),
and the setting for the tabernacle,
teba, candelabra and chandeliers.

The vaults of Cathédrale Ste-Anne

10 Cathédrale Ste-Anne, Apt
MAP C3 ▪ Pl de la Cathédrale
▪ Open Nov–Apr: 10am–noon &
2–5pm Tue–Sat; May–Oct: 9am–
1pm & 3–6pm Tue–Sat (except during
religious ceremonies)

The relics of St Anne (mother of the
Virgin),discovered on this site in 776,
remain here, having survived the
destruction of the church and its
rebuilding from the 11th century on.
The two crypts have also survived,
containing sarcophagi from early
Christian times. The cathedral has
18th-century paintings and a 15th-
century stained-glass window of
the Tree of Jesse. The St Anne
Chapel contains what is rumoured
to be the saint's veil.

A DAY'S DRIVE IN THE VAUCLUSE MOUNTAINS

[Map showing: Séguret, Dentelles de Montmirail, Malaucène, Mont Ventoux, Col des Tempêtes, D974, Les Lavandes, Monieux, Mazan, Sault, Carpentras, Villes-sur-Auzon, Gorges de la Nesque, D942]

▶ MORNING

Start in Carpentras by visiting
the **Synagogue**. Take the
D942 to Mazan and on, through
woodland, to Villes-sur-Auzon,
a charming Provençal village.
Continue on the D942 to the
Gorges de la Nesque to experience 20 km (12 miles) of awe-
inspiring scenery, with sheer
drops of 300 m (1,000 ft). Pause
at the Belvédère de Castelleras
for heart-stopping views.

Continue to Monieux, stopping at
Les Lavandes restaurant (04 90
64 05 08; €) in the village centre if
it is time for lunch and you fancy
elegant, classic cooking. Continue
to **Sault** (see p46) where, in July
and August, the valley is a riot
of purple lavender, yellow broom
and the white of the rocks – an
unmissable sight.

AFTERNOON

Take the D164 towards **Mont
Ventoux** (see p125), another
challenging drive, and stop for a
break at the Col des Tempêtes.
Take in the amazing views across
Toulourenc Valley, then journey
the summit for the most stunning
panorama in Provence.

Descend the mountain to
Malaucène, taking the tiny D90
into the **Dentelles de Montmirail**.
Pause in any of the cafés in
Beaumes-de-Venise for a glass
of the local sweet white wine.
Continue to delightful **Séguret**
(see p49), then return by the D7 to
Carpentras, rewarding yourself
with dinner at **Le Mesclun** (rue
des Poternes; 04 90 46 93 43; €€),
the best restaurant in town.

Avignon Sights

 1 Cathédrale Notre-Dame-des-Doms

MAP B3 ■ Pl du Palais ■ Open 8am–6pm daily (7am–7pm summer)

The medieval popes' cathedral has 17th-century alterations but a 13th-century altar.

 2 Place de l'Horloge

MAP B3

Built on the old forum, the city's nerve centre is fringed with restaurants, bars and the 19th-century town hall.

3 Chartreuse du Val-de-Bénédiction

MAP B3 ■ 58 rue de la République, Villeneuve-lez-Avignon ■ Open Apr–Sep: 9:30am–6:30pm daily; Oct–Mar: 10am–5pm daily ■ Closed 1 Jan, 1 May, 1 & 11 Nov, 25 Dec, 2 weeks Jan ■ Adm

An impressive monastery and chapel with elegant gardens.

4 Musée Angladon-Collection Jacques Doucet

MAP B3 ■ 5 rue Laboureur ■ Open Apr–Oct: 1–6pm Tue–Sun; Nov–Mar: 1–6pm Tue–Sat ■ Closed 1 Jan, 25 Dec ■ Adm

This private collection includes fabulous works by Cézanne, Manet, Picasso and Van Gogh.

5 Palais des Papes

The medieval papal palace (see pp12–13) dominates the town.

Panorama of the Palais des Papes

 **6 Pont St-Bénézet**

MAP B3 ■ Bd de la Ligne ■ Open daily; Mar: 9am–6:30pm; Apr–Jun & Sep–Oct: 9am–7pm (to 8pm Jul, to 8:30pm Aug); Nov–Feb: 9:30am–5:45pm ■ Adm

This 12th-century bridge (see p46) once had 22 arches, now it has four.

7 Rue des Teinturiers

MAP B3

This tiny street – formerly home to dye-workers – now buzzes with arty cafés and quirky boutiques.

8 Musée du Petit Palais

MAP B3 ■ Pl du Palais ■ Open 10am–1pm, 2–6pm Wed–Mon ■ Closed 1 Jan, 1 May, 25 Dec ■ Adm

This superb collection of medieval and Renaissance art includes an early painting by Botticelli.

9 Collection Lambert

MAP B3 ■ Musée d'Art Contemporain, 5 rue Violette ■ Open 11am–6pm Tue–Sun (to 7pm daily Jul–Aug) ■ Adm

This is Avignon's premier showcase for contemporary art.

10 Musée Calvet

MAP B3 ■ 65 rue Joseph Vernet ■ Open 10am–1pm, 2–6pm Wed–Mon ■ Closed 1 Jan, 1 May, 25 Dec ■ www.musee-calvet.org ■ Adm

The Calvet is a fine museum, with collections of paintings, sculptures and artifacts from ancient Greece to the 20th century.

Vaucluse Villages

 1 Séguret
MAP C2

This remarkably pretty medieval settlement hugs the hillside like a tight belt *(see p49)*. Gorgeous views.

 2 Gordes
MAP C3 ▪ www.gordes-village.com

Fashionable folk flock here, and no wonder. The village is perched above the Coulon Valley, and its little houses appear piled on top of one another. In the centre, the château oversees the whole with a stately Renaissance dignity.

 3 Oppède-le-Vieux
MAP C3

Flourishing in Renaissance times, Oppède was deserted by 1900 – no one wanted to live on a barely accessible rock. Now its houses are being restored by creative types, such as artists and writers, but the spot remains profoundly atmospheric, with medieval castle ruins.

4 Brantes
MAP C2

Overhanging the gorges 550 m (1,800 ft) below, Brantes stares across the Toulourenc Valley to Mont Ventoux. Its tiny paved streets and vaulted passages boast a chapel but no shops. It is particularly impressive in March, when the almond trees are in bloom.

5 Malaucène
MAP C2

This was where Pope Clement V had his summer residence, and it remains a grand place of 17th- and 18th-century houses, fountains and avenues shaded by plane trees.

6 Vacqueyras
MAP B2

One of Provence's most prestigious wine villages. Admire the 11th-century church with its elegant bell tower, then go to taste the wine.

 7 Ansouis
MAP C3 ▪ Château: call 04 90 77 23 36 for information on tours; adm

This village, with its labyrinthe of narrow streets, is made truly remarkable by its château, built in the 1100s and lived in by the same family until the early 2000s. The vaulted rooms, salons, armoury and kitchens are extraordinary, as are the stately gardens.

The hilltop village of Ansouis

 8 Roussillon
MAP C3

Ochre mining and erosion have fashioned the multicoloured earth into cliffs *(see p49)* and fantastic shapes, creating a bewitching setting for a romantic perched village.

9 Ménerbes
MAP C3

Ménerbes was superbly sited for defence. As a Protestant stronghold, it held out for five years during the 16th-century Wars of Religion. The position remains dramatic, but peace now reigns around the citadel and town houses. The views are terrific.

10 Le Barroux
MAP C2

This eagle's nest of a village has narrow streets leading steeply up to the splendid château at the top.

See map on pp124–5 ←

Shops in Vaucluse

L'Isle-sur-la-Sorgue
MAP C3

Not one shop but more than 200 make this little town France's most important antiques and second-hand centre, after Paris. Grouped into seven centres, most are open Saturday to Monday, with a market on Sunday mornings. Antiques fairs are at Easter and around All Saint's Day.

L'Isle-sur-la-Sorgue market

2 Farmers' Market, Velleron
MAP C3

Provence isn't short of food markets, but this one is special. It's held in the evening and stall-holders must sell homegrown or raised produce only. It is held Monday to Saturday from 6pm, April to September, and Tuesday, Wednesday, Friday and Saturday from 4:30pm the rest of the year.

3 Les Délices du Luberon, L'Isle-sur-la-Sorgue
MAP C3 ▪ 1 av du Partage des Eaux

An unprepossessing warehouse that is full of olives, olive preparations and olive derivatives such as tapenade or *melet* (a blend of fennel, peppers, olives and anchovies).

4 Lou Canesteou, Vaison-la-Romaine
MAP C2 ▪ 10 rue Raspail

Josiane Déal personally selects the 160 varieties of artisanal cheese for her shop, and has been named a *Meilleur Ouvrier* ("Master of her Craft") for her expertise.

5 Olivades, Avignon
MAP B3 ▪ 56 rue Joseph Vernet

This company has been producing and printing Provençal fabrics since 1818. It's now the only such outfit in the region, with materials, table linen and wedding gowns.

6 Edith Mézard, Goult
MAP C3 ▪ Château de l'Ange

The little château near Goult is a perfect setting for beautifully embroidered clothes and a great range of linen for the house.

7 Confiserie Artisanale Denis Ceccon, Apt
MAP C3 ▪ 24 quai de la Liberté

Apt is the world capital of crystallized fruit, and Denis Ceccon is one of the few remaining artisans to work by traditional methods – try the apricots.

8 Nougats Silvain, St-Didier
MAP C3 ▪ 4 pl Neuve

This is a farming and fruit-growing family known for the delicious nougat. Don't miss the honey either.

9 Château Pesquié, Mormoiron
MAP C2 ▪ 1365 bis rte de Flassan

The château has lovely grounds and first-rate Ventoux wines.

10 Chocolaterie Bernard Castelain, Châteauneuf-du-Pape
MAP B3 ▪ 1745 rte de Sorgues

Another warehouse – this time packed with a dazzling array of chocolate. Enter only if you have iron self-control.

Chocolaterie Bernard Castelain

Places to Eat

PRICE CATEGORIES

For a three-course meal for one with half a bottle of wine (or equivalent meal), taxes and extra charges.

€ under €40 €€ €40–€60 €€€ over €60

1 La Bastide de Capelongue, Bonnieux

MAP C3 ■ Les Claparèdes, chemin des Cabanes ■ 04 90 75 89 78 ■ Closed Tue, Wed L mid-Jan–early Mar, 2 weeks Dec ■ €€€

Chef Noël Bérard is known for aromatic Provençal cuisine, using his own herbs for dishes such as rack of lamb smoked with wild thyme.

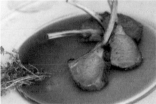

Lamb at La Bastide de Capelongue

2 Café Fleurs, L'Isle-sur-la-Sorgue

MAP C3 ■ 9 rue Théodore Aubanel ■ 09 54 12 31 29 ■ Closed Mon, Tue (excl mid-Jun–Aug), Jan ■ €€

Delicious Provençal food served in a stylish dining room or on a shady patio.

3 Hiély Lucullus, Avignon

MAP B3 ■ 5 rue de la République ■ 04 90 86 17 07 ■ Closed Tue, Wed ■ €€

One of Avignon's oldest restaurants, which adds a wonderful lightness of touch to its classic dishes.

4 Chez Serge, Carpentras

MAP C3 ■ 90 rue Cottier ■ 04 90 63 21 24 ■ €€

Chef Serge's elegant, modern bistro is acclaimed for its good-value Provençal dishes. The wine and truffle evenings are especially popular.

5 Les Florets, Gigondas

MAP B2 ■ 1243 rte des Florêts ■ 04 90 65 85 01 ■ Closed Wed, Jan–mid-Mar ■ €€

The panoramic terrace has superb views of the Dentelles de Montmirail, and the regional cuisine is matched by an excellent wine list.

6 Restaurant Sevin, Avignon

MAP B3 ■ 10 rue de Mons ■ 04 90 86 16 50 ■ 04 90 86 16 50 ■ Closed Wed, Thu ■ €€€

Tasting menus of superb Provençal fare are matched with excellent wines at this esteemed restaurant.

7 Auberge la Fenière, Lourmarin

MAP C3 ■ Rte de Lourmarin ■ 04 90 68 11 79 ■ Closed Mon, Tue (Jul & Aug: open D), mid-Nov–early Feb ■ €€

Nadia Sammut, one of France's rare female top chefs, brings international influence to regional cuisine.

8 Le Prieuré, Villeneuve-lès-Avignon

MAP B3 ■ 7 pl du Chapitre ■ 04 90 15 90 15 ■ Closed Nov–Mar ■ €€€

The locally sourced menu changes four times a week, offering gourmet cuisine in a heavenly setting.

9 Moulin à Huile, Le Vaison-la-Romaine

MAP C2 ■ 1 quai Maréchal Foch ■ 04 90 36 04 56 ■ Closed Tue, Wed ■ €€€

Superb setting in the medieval part of town. The chefs prepare excellent regional dishes for a set menu.

10 La Fourchette, Avignon

MAP B3 ■ 17 rue Racine ■ 04 90 85 20 93 ■ Closed Sat, Sun, 3 wks Aug ■ €€

Much favoured by Avignon locals for its country-inn style and treatment of Provençal classics, like sumptuous *boeuf en daube (see p67).*

See map on pp124–5

Streetsmart

Colourful façades of houses in the city of Orange, Vaucluse

Getting Around

Arriving by Air

Provence has five international airports in Avignon, Marseille, Nice, Nîmes and Toulon-Hyères; all are near their respective cities, with good bus services to the city centres.

Nice Airport is the main gateway for Provence, with the most frequent flights from Paris, London, New York and other major cities. Buses run the 7 km (4.5 miles) to central Nice every 15 minutes. A taxi to the city centre costs around €40. Other direct airport buses regularly serve Antibes, Cannes and Monaco.

Marseille Airport is situated 25 km (16 miles) northwest of Marseille and 28 km (17 miles) southwest of Aix-en-Provence. Taxis to both destinations cost around €55. Buses run to Marseille-St-Charles railway station about every 15 minutes, and numerous other direct buses serve Aix-en-Provence, St-Tropez and other cities and town in inland Provence.

Avignon Airport is 10 km (6 miles) from the city centre. A taxi or LER bus takes 40 minutes from the airport to central Avignon. Nîmes Airport is 13 km (8 miles) from Nîmes, and a taxi or Navette Aéroport coach will take you to the city in 15 minutes. Toulon-Hyères Airport is 24 km (15 miles) from Toulon and 8 km (5 miles) from Hyères; the Réseau Mistral bus takes 30 minutes and 20 minutes, respectively, to reach the city centres.

Monaco has no airport but has a city centre heliport with a helicopter shuttle service to Nice International Airport, taking seven minutes with **Héli Securité.**

International Train Travel

High-speed TGV trains connect Provence with the UK, Italy, Spain and Switzerland. Most TGV stations are conveniently located in city centres except for Avignon and Aix-en-Provence whose airport-style TGV stations are a short bus ride from the town centre. **Eurostar** services run directly from London to Avignon and Marseille, the latter a six-and-a-half-hour service. Reservations for all TGV services are essential as tickets are booked up quickly. Visit the **RENFE-SNCF** or **Oui SNCF** websites for tickets, depending on your route.

You can buy tickets and passes for multiple international journeys via **Eurail** or **Interrail**; however, you may need to pay an additional reservation fee. Check carefully before boarding that your pass is valid on the service you wish to use.

Students and those under 26 and over 60 can benefit from discounted rail travel both to and within France. For more information on discounted travel, visit the Eurail or Interrail websites.

Regional and Local Trains

Provence is a vast geographical region covered by mountains, lakes and rolling fields of lavender. Fortunately, every major town is connected by high-speed TGV trains, run by the French rail operator **SNCF**. The line goes from Arles and Nîmes in the west to Nice and Monaco in the east. Even tiny villages are linked by **TER**, also operated by SNCF, which serves every station on local and suburban routes.

It is not essential to reserve your journey in advance on regional and local trains, but advance purchase is a good idea at the height of the tourist season in summer.

The narrow-gauge **Train des Pignes** is a popular journey. This historic route runs from Nice's Gare de Provence to Digne-les-Bains in the Haut-Alpes through splendid Alpine scenery. Several walking trails begin at stations en route.

The **Train des Merveilles** is another pretty route, particularly attrictive to hikers. The line runs from Nice deep into the Italian Alps through what was Italian territory until 1947, past the towns of Tende and Sospel.

There are frequent links between many Provençal cities and Paris. It is a three-hour journey from the French capital to Marseille, Avignon or Aix-en-Provence.

Long-Distance Bus Travel

BlaBlaCar coaches connect many cities in Provence, including Marseille and Nîmes, with Paris, Lyon, Montpellier, Toulouse and Bordeaux. **Flixbus** connects cities in Provence with Paris, as well as with other French towns and major European destinations.

Public Transport

Each urban area in Provence has its own public transport system extending from the city centre to the outer suburbs. Safety and hygiene measures, timetables, ticket information, transport maps and more can be obtained from their respective websites.

City Transport

The region's cities have efficient transport networks. **Orizo** is the local transport authority for Avignon and its suburbs, including Villeneuvelès-Avignon. Hop-on, hop-off electric shuttle buses (Baladines) trundle around the medieval centre.

In Marseille, **RTM** co-ordinates bus, Métro and tram lines. **CAM** operates buses within Monaco and to Nice and Menton, and seven lifts and escalators connect its waterfront with the upper urban level. **Lignes d'Azur** is the public transport operator for Nice, Cannes and Alpes-Maritimes, including the Nice tramway. **Réseau Mistral**

is Toulon's city and suburban public bus and boat bus network.

Tickets

Buying tickets in advance is always cheaper than buying from the driver. *Carnets* (books of up to ten tickets) and multi-trip passes valid for one or more days are available on all urban transport networks and can be bought at rail and bus stations, designated stores and city tourist information offices. Remember to always purchase a ticket as ticket inspections are quite common.

Local Buses

Beyond major towns, local bus routes are served by private companies under regional authority governance. Timetables are geared to the needs of local schools and shoppers, and do not always present the best choice for visitors. **ZOU!** is the one-stop shop for local buses across the region.

Trams

Trams can be more efficient than buses in Provence's cities. Marseille's tramway operates over three lines, and tickets must be purchased in advance. Nice has a three-route tram system and tickets can be bought from machines at the tramstop. Tickets for Avignon's trams can be bought from machines at tram stations or via the Orizo smartphone app.

Taxis

There are taxi ranks at rail and bus stations, airports and in most main squares in towns and cities. You can also call or text for taxis. **Cab Express Taxi Moto** are motorbike taxis in Nice. A list of key taxi firms is shown in the Directory box.

Driving to Provence

It takes nine to ten hours to drive to Avignon from the Channel ferry ports via the A26 and A27 *autoroutes*. Driving from Bilbao in Spain, which is served by ferries from the UK, takes around eight hours. The drive from Paris to Provence is an easy one, except at the start or end of French holiday periods. Allow at least six hours for the 700-km (435-mile) journey to Avignon via the A6 Autoroute du Soleil, as well as about €60 in tolls. From Paris to Nice allow ten hours plus around €80 in tolls. There are rest stops, or *aires*, every 30 km (20 miles) or so. Most have picnictables and public toilets.

To take your own car into France, you will need proof of registration, valid insurance documents, a full, valid driving licence and your passport.

Car Rental

To rent a car in France you must be 21 years or over and have held a valid driver's licence for at least a year. You will also need to present a credit card. Driving licences issued by any of the EU member states are valid throughout the EU. International driving licences are not needed for short-term visitors (up to 90 days) from the UK, North America, Australia and New Zealand. Visitors from other countries should check with their automobile association.

All the main car hire companies have offices in Provençal towns. Nice has an all-electric car share scheme **Mobilize Share**.

Driving in Provence

Driving in Provence can be a pleasure, but plan your journey carefully to avoid traffic bottlenecks on rural and coastal roads in summer.

For a fast point-to-point journey, the A8 *autoroute* cuts across the Camargue from Menton to Aix-en-Provence, near which it meets the A7 Autoroute du Soleil, so you can drive on *autoroutes* all the way across Provence from the Italian border to Orange in just over three hours. The same journey avoiding *autoroutes* takes more than six hours but costs less, as the A8 is the most expensive toll road in France.

Routes départementales are the narrowest and slowest roads, but in hinterland regions such as Alpes-de-Hautes-Provence they may be your only option. **Bison Futé** signs indicate routes avoiding heavy traffic and can be useful during peak French holiday periods.

Driving in the historic centres of Provençal towns is not recommended. Finding your way isn't easy as there are many one-way streets, and parking is difficult and expensive. In summer, traffic on the coast road between Hyères and Nice, and especially the section between Nice and Cannes, is often excruciatingly slow.

Rules of the Road

Always drive on the right. Unless otherwise signposted, vehicles coming from the right have right of way, and cars on a roundabout usually have right of way as well.

At all times, drivers must carry a valid driver's licence and registration and insurance documents. In case of a breakdown, it is compulsory to carry a red warning triangle and a luminous vest. Seat belts must be worn, and it is prohibited to sound your horn in cities except in a genuine emergency. For motorbikes and scooters, the wearing of helmets and protective gloves is compulsory. It is against the law to drive in urban bus lanes. France strictly enforces its drink-drive limit *(p138)*, and random breath testing at mobile checkpoints is common.

Parking

Park only in areas with a large "P" or a Payant sign on the pavement or road, and pay at the parking meter with cash or contactless debit or credit card. Avignon, Marseille, Nice and Toulon have numerous underground car parks, signposted by a white "P" on a blue background, and overground car parks are usually located on the edge of historic town centres. Some city hotels have private parking.

Boats and Ferries

Boats are a great way to take a day trip along the coast. Most useful are the **Trans Côte d'Azur** ferries from Cannes to the Îles de Lérins, and **Bateaux Verts** from Ste-Maxime to St-Tropez. Boat tours are also run around Avignon and into the Camargue.

The free *navette fluviale* (river shuttle), also known as the *bac à traille*, crosses the Rhône between the Quai de la Ligne in central Avignon and Île de la Barthelasse. Réseau Mistral *(p135)* runs *bateau-bus* (water taxi) services from Toulon to La Seyne-sur-Mer and Les Sablettes. **Bateliers de la Côte d'Azur** sail from Toulon to the Îles d'Hyères. Ferries from Marseille's Vieux Port to Pointe-Rouge and l'Estaque are operated by RTM *(p135)*. In Monaco, CAM bus-boats *(p135)* link Quai Kennedy with the cruise ship terminal.

Corsica Linea sails from Marseille to Corsica, Sardinia, Algeria and Tunisia. **Corsica Ferries** sail from Nice and Toulon to Corsica and Sardinia and from Toulon to Majorca and Sicily.

Cycling

Most towns (except Nice and Monaco) have few hills and bike rentals are widely available. In the hot summer months, or for less energetic riders, electric-boosted e-bikes take less effort.

Vélopop' in Avignon, **Le Vélo** in Marseille and **Vélobleu** in Nice are bike-sharing schemes. Register online first, and then grab a bike from one of the multiple docking stations around each city. Aix-en-Provence doesn't have a bike-sharing scheme, but **Aixprit Vélo** is a handy bike shop that also rents out bikes in the city.

Bicycles may be taken on most trains, but the service must be booked in advance on TGV trains. To take your bike on a local train, look for the bicycle symbol on the timetable. Wearing a helmet is not compulsory but is strongly advised.

Walking

Provence is superb walking country, offering guided or marked walks around historic cities and along the coast.

Sentiers balisés are the local trails, while *sentiers de grande randonnée* are long-distance hiking tracks, and both are part of a vast network that covers all of France. The main long-distance trails are the GR5, GR51, GR6 and GR9. Maps and guides are widely available from tourist offices.

The most rewarding way to take in any city and absorb its atmosphere is on foot. In many cities, sights are only a short distance apart.

DIRECTORY

TAXIS

Cab Express Taxi-Moto
🕸 cab-express.com

Provence Cab (Avignon)
🕸 provencecab-paca.fr

Taxi Cannes
🕸 taxi-cannes.net

Taxi Monaco
🕸 taximonaco.com

Taxi Radio Marseille
🕸 taximarseille.com

Taxi Riviera Nice
🕸 taxis-nice.fr

Taxi Toulon
🕸 taxi-toulon.com

CAR RENTAL

Mobilize Share
🕸 fr.share.mobilize.com

DRIVING IN PROVENCE

Bison Futé
🕸 bison-fute.gouv.fr

BOATS AND FERRIES

Bateau Verts
🕸 bateauxverts.com

Bateliers de la Côte d'Azur
🕸 bateliersdelacotedazur.com

Corsica Ferries
🕸 corsica-ferries.fr

Corsica Linea
🕸 corsicalinea.com

Trans Côte d'Azur
🕸 trans-cote-azur.com

CYCLING

Aixprit Vélo'
🕸 aixpritvelo.com

Le Vélo
🕸 levelo-mpm.fr

Vélobleu
🕸 velobleu.org

Vélopop'
🕸 velopop.fr

Practical Information

Passports and Visas

For entry requirements, including visas, consult your nearest French embassy or check the **France-Visas** website. Visitors from outside the European Economic Area (EEA), European Union (EU) and Switzerland need a valid passport to enter France. EEA, EU and Swiss nationals can use their national identity cards instead. Citizens of the UK, Canada, the US, Australia and New Zealand can visit France for up to three months without a visa as long as their passport is valid for six months beyond the date of entry. For longer stays, a visa is required and must be obtained in advance from the French Embassy in your home country. Most other non-EU nationals need a visa. Schengen visas are valid for France.

Government Advice

Now more than ever, it is important to consult both your and the French government's advice before travelling. The **UK Foreign and Commonwealth Office**, the **US Department of State**, the **Australian Department of Foreign Affairs and Trade** and **Gouvernement France** offer all the latest information on security, health and local regulations.

Customs Information

You can find information on the laws relating to goods and currency taken in or out of France on the **Douanes et Droits Indirects** website. For EU citizens there is no limit on most goods, as long as the items are for your personal use.

Insurance

We recommend that you take out a comprehensive insurance policy covering theft, loss of belongings, medical care, cancellations and delays, and read the small print carefully. EU and UK citizens are eligible for free emergency medical care provided they have a valid European Health Insurance Card (**EHIC**) or a UK Global Health Insurance Card (**GHIC**). Visitors from outside the EU must arrange their own private medical insurance.

Health

France has a world-class healthcare system. Emergency medical care is free for all UK and EU nationals. If you have an EHIC or GHIC, be sure to present this as soon as possible. You may have to pay for treatment and reclaim the money later. For other visitors, payment of medical expenses is the patient's responsibility. It is therefore important to arrange comprehensive medical insurance before travelling.

SOS Médecins is a 24-hour medical service, which provides general medical, emergency and out-of-hours visits at your hotel. If you need an ambulance, dial 112.

A green cross indicates a pharmacy. Pharmacists are an excellent source of advice – they can diagnose many health problems and suggest appropriate treatment. Phone 3237 to find the nearest pharmacy. They are usually open from 9am to 8pm Monday to Saturday. When closed, there will be a sign in the window giving the location of the nearest *pharmacie de nuit*, which will be open. In all towns one pharmacy will open at night and weekends. Some pharmacies are open 24/7.

No inoculations are needed for France. For information regarding COVID-19 vaccination requirements, consult government advice. Tap water in France is safe to drink, unless otherwise stated.

Provence has its share of pests, from mosquitoes to jellyfish, and beware of spiky sea urchins when walking on rocky shores.

Smoking, Alcohol and Drugs

Smoking is prohibited in all public places, but is allowed on open-air restaurant, café and bar terraces. The possession of illegal drugs is prohibited and could result in a prison sentence. Unless stated otherwise, alcohol consumption on the streets is permitted. France has a strict limit of 0.05 per cent BAC (blood alcohol content) for drivers.

ID

There is no requirement for visitors to carry ID, but in the event of a routine check you may be asked to show your passport. If you don't have it with you, the police may escort you to wherever your passport is being kept.

Personal Security

Provence is generally a safe region, though petty crime can take place. Beware of pickpockets and bag-snatchers on public transport, especially during rush hour and in major tourist areas. Use your commonsense and be alert to your surroundings, and you should have a trouble-free trip. If you have anything stolen, report the crime as soon as possible to the nearest police station, and bring ID with you. Get a copy of the crime report in order to claim on your insurance. Contact your embassy or consulate if your passport is stolen, or in the event of a serious crime or accident.

For emergency **police**, **ambulance** or **fire** services dial 112 – the operator will ask which service you require. For ambulance emergencies you can also dial 15; for the fire brigade the direct number is 18; and for the police the number is 17.

Like the rest of France, Provence is diverse and multicultural. As a rule, Provençals are accepting of all people regardless of their race, gender or sexuality although rural Provence tends to be more conservative than the big cities. Same-sex marriage was legalized in 2013 and France recognized the right to legally change your gender in 2016. Nice, Cannes, Aix-en-Provence and especially Marseille have thriving LGBTQ+ communities. Gay Map Marseille lists bars, restaurants, clubs and other attractions in Marseille and Aix-en-Provence.

Travellers with Specific Requirements

Most museums are wheelchair-accessible and offer audio tours and induction loops. **Bespoke Holidays** specializes in accommodation for wheelchair users and people with learning disabilities and their carers. Fully supported activity holidays are offered by **Go Beyond**.

To find out about accessible public transport and attractions in Nice, download the handy Nice Accessible PDF from the **Office de Tourisme Nice** website. National train operator SNCF offers **Accès Plus**, which accompanies travellers with specific needs on rail journeys.

DIRECTORY

PASSPORTS AND VISAS

France-Visas
🔳 france-visas.gouv.fr

GOVERNMENT ADVICE

Australian Department of Foreign Affairs and Trade
🔳 smarttraveller.gov.au

Gouvernement France
🔳 gouvernement.fr

UK Foreign and Commonwealth Office
🔳 gov.uk/foreign-travel-advice

US Department of State
🔳 travel.state.gov

CUSTOMS INFORMATION

Douanes et Droits Indirects
🔳 douane.gouv.fr

INSURANCE

EHIC
🔳 ec.europa.eu

GHIC
🔳 ghic.org.uk

HEALTH

SOS Médecins
📞 sosmedecinsfrance.fr

PERSONAL SECURITY

Ambulance
📞 15

Fire
📞 18

Police
📞 17

Police, Ambulance, Fire
📞 112

TRAVELLERS WITH SPECIFIC REQUIREMENTS

Accès Plus
🔳 accessibilite.sncf.com

Accès Plus
🔳 accessibilite.sncf.com

Bespoke Holidays
🔳 bespokefrance.com

Go Beyond
🔳 gobeyondholidays.com

Office de Tourisme Nice
🔳 nicetourisme.com/nice-accessible

Time Zone

France operates Central European Time (CET). The clock moves forward by one hour during European Daylight Savings Time, which runs from the last Sunday in March until the last Sunday in October.

Money

France uses the euro (€). Most establishments accept major credit, debit and pre-paid currency cards. Contactless payments are accepted in major cities. Most taxi drivers and market traders, as well as many smaller bars and restaurants, accept only cash, so do carry a small amount with you.

Tipping waiters in restaurants is considered polite. If you are pleased with the service, a tip of 5–10 per cent of the total bill is appreciated. Hotel porters and housekeeping generally expect a tip of €1 to €2 per bag or day. For taxi journeys, round up the fare to the nearest euro.

Electrical Appliances

Standard voltage in France is 230V. Power sockets are type C and E, fitting two-pronged plugs. You will need adaptors, and possibly a transformer (for some US electrical appliances).

Mobile Phones and Wi-Fi

Free Wi-Fi hotspots are available in a number of public spaces, including museums, libraries and parks. Almost all hotels and many cafés and restaurants offer free Wi-Fi for patrons.

Visitors with EU mobile phone contracts can use their devices in Provence without additional data roaming charges. Users will be charged the same rates for data, SMS and voice calls as they would pay at home. Those not on EU tariffs should check roaming rates with their provider. A cheaper option may be to purchase a French SIM card (you will need to show ID).

Mobile phone coverage in most cities, towns and villages is good but mobile and GPS reception in some mountainous areas is patchy.

Postal Services

Stamps (timbres) can be bought at post offices and tabacs (tobacconists) or online via **La Poste**. Most post offices have self-service machines to weigh and frank your mail. Yellow post boxes are ubiquitous.

Weather

The south of France, and especially the Côte d'Azur, is justly famed for having one of the most desirable climates on the planet. The coastal stretches from Monaco to Cannes bathe in up to 300 days of sun per year. Pleasant breezes keep most of the sweltering summer heat at bay during the busy months of July and August, although visitors should be prepared for an occasional week-long heat wave, which makes sightseeing a little more arduous. Temperatures in May, June, September and October usually hover around 25°C (77°F). Restaurant terraces will be busy but fewer crowds descend upon the region's cultural sights. November and March can be rainy. The sunshine makes even midwinter a terrific time to visit, but bear in mind that Mistral winds can bring icy weather to Marseille and inland Provence.

For two weeks in May it becomes impossible to get a hotel room or a table in a good restaurant in or around Cannes as the resort hosts its Film Festival. The same is true of Monaco when the Rallye Monte-Carlo (Jan) and Monaco Grand Prix (dates vary) take place.

August sees long delays on the roads to and around the south – avoid the first and last weekends.

Opening Hours

COVID-19 Increased rates of infection may result in temporary opening hours and/or closures. Always check ahead before visiting museums, attractions and hospitality venues.

In general, big stores and supermarkets open from 8am to 7pm, plus 9am to 1pm on Sundays. Many smaller shops and businesses close for an hour or two from around noon and are closed on Sundays and public holidays. Very few restaurants serve lunch after 2pm.

Museums have similar opening hours across the entire region. Almost all are open from 10am to

6pm Tuesday to Sunday. Outdoor cultural sights stay open later in summer.

Visitor Information

Multilingual staff can offer advice on where to visit, and hand out a wealth of maps and brochures, at every Office de Tourisme in Provence and the Côte d'Azur. Even the tiniest town has an informative, all-encompassing website with sightseeing ideas and accommodation information in several languages. The websites of larger cities, such as **Nice Tourisme** and **Marseille Tourisme**, offer a selection of tourism, transport and children's apps, plus downloadable PDF brochures.

The wider official web portals for **MyProvence** and **Côte d'Azur Tourisme** offer plenty of information and tempting ideas, such as sea-kayaking in the Camargue and vineyard visits in the Var.

City and regional passes can help you cut the cost of sightseeing and public transport. The **Avignon City Pass**, valid for 24 or 48 hours, offers free access to museums, monuments and gardens in Avignon and Villeneuve-lès-Avignon, as well as official themed guided tours. The **Vaucluse Provence Pass**, valid for two, three or five days, covers the wider Vaucluse region. The **French Riviera Pass** allows free access to many sights, tours and activities, and free travel on public transport throughout the Nice-Côte d'Azur metropolitan area. The **Marseille CityPass** includes free public transport, free admission to museums and galleries and other discounts.

Local Customs

Étiquette (la politesse) is important to the French. Upon entering a store or café you are expected to say bonjour and, when leaving, to say au revoir to staff. Be sure to add s'il vous plaît (please) when ordering and pardon (sorry) if you accidentally bump into someone.

The French usually shake hands when meeting someone for the first time. Friends and colleagues who know each other well will greet each other with a kiss on each cheek. If you are unsure about what's expected, wait to see if they offer a hand or a cheek.

When visiting churches and cathedrals, dress respectfully and keep mobile phones on silent.

Language

French is the official language spoken in France. English is spoken in large hotels, but not in all smaller establishments, shops, bars and cafés, so mastering a few niceties goes a long way.

Taxes and Refunds

A sales tax (TVA) of 20 per cent is imposed on most goods and services. Non-EU residents can reclaim the TVA they pay on French goods at shops displaying the Global Refund Tax-Free sign as long as they spend more than €175 in the same shop in one day, and take the goods out of France. The retailer will generally supply a form and issue a détaxe receipt at the time of purchase. Make sure that you have your passport with you to prove non-resident status.

Accommodation

Gîtes de France lists almost 2,500 rural self-catering holiday rental properties, chambres d'hôtes (B&Bs) and campsites in Provence. Book well ahead if you plan to visit in summer (June to August) or during events such as the Avignon Festival or Cannes Film Festival.

Places to Stay

PRICE CATEGORIES

For a standard, double room per night (with breakfast if included), taxes and extra charges.

€ under €200   €€ 200–400   €€€ over €400

Luxury Resorts

Hôtel la Baie Dorée, Antibes

MAP G4 ▪ 579 bd de la Garoupe ▪ 04 93 67 30 67 ▪ www.baiedoree.com ▪ €€

With only 15 rooms – all but two of which have a view of the sea – this hotel is an intimate alternative to the usual large-scale luxury resorts found on the Riviera. It has a private beach and a jetty with loungers set around a tiny harbour.

Cap Estel, Eze

MAP H4 ▪ 1312 av Raymond Poincaré, Èze ▪ 04 93 76 29 29 ▪ www. capestel.com ▪ €€€

Constructed in 1900 on a secluded peninsula with a private beach, the Cap Estel is much-loved by A-listers for its pampering and privacy. Rooms are in four buildings amid an exotic garden with a spectacular infinity pool.

Hôtel Martinez, Cannes

MAP G4 ▪ 73 bd de la Croisette ▪ 04 93 90 12 34 ▪ www.hyatt.com ▪ €€€

A landmark on Cannes' esplanade, the Martinez is a triumph of fin-de-siècle wedding-cake stucco architecture, with a private beach. Part of the Hyatt chain of luxury hotels, it has everything you could want for a sybaritic stay.

Le Byblos, St-Tropez

MAP F5 ▪ 20 av Paul Signac ▪ 04 94 56 68 00 ▪ Closed Nov–Mar ▪ www.byblos.com ▪ €€€

Beloved of rock stars and fashionistas, Le Byblos also has one of St-Trop's trendiest nightspots, Les Caves du Roy (see p92), attached to it. There's also a Sisley spa and a poolside restaurant. Decked out in Art Deco colours worthy of a chic fashion shoot, this is among the most luxurious hotels in Provence.

Monte Carlo Beach Hotel, Roquebrune-Cap-Martin

MAP H3 ▪ Av Princesse-Grace ▪ 04 93 28 66 66 ▪ www.montecarlosbm. com ▪ €€€

This 46-room Art Deco showpiece hotel has an Olympic-sized pool, a crescent of private beach, three fine restaurants and an overall ambience of exclusive luxury and comfort.

Cheval Blanc, St-Tropez

MAP F5 ▪ Plage de la Bouillabaisse ▪ 04 94 55 91 00 ▪ Closed mid-Oct–mid-Apr ▪ www.cheval blanc.com ▪ €€€

With its private beach, pool, fine sea views and excellent location, it is hardly surprising that this is a favourite with those who know St-Tropez well.

Grand Hotels

Carlton Inter-Continental, Cannes

MAP G4 ▪ 58 La Croisette ▪ 04 93 06 40 06 ▪ www. intercontinental-carlton-cannes.com ▪ €€

The Carlton is a Cannes landmark, home of the stars during the Film Festival and appropriately luxurious, with its private beach and high standards of service. The hotel is closed for renovations until spring 2023, but its chic beach club remains open (see p109).

Hôtel d'Europe, Avignon

MAP B3 ▪ 12 pl Crillon ▪ 04 90 14 76 76 ▪ www. heurope.com ▪ €€

Step back in time as you enter the ornate gates of this beautiful, historic hotel. Heavy wooden furniture and antique tapestries create an elegant atmosphere, and no request is too much for the impeccable staff.

Hôtel Hermitage, Monte Carlo

MAP H4 ▪ Sq Beaumarchais ▪ 00 377 98 06 40 00 ▪ www.monte carlosbm.com ▪ €€

Despite its sleek, contemporary Yannick Alléno restaurant and the Mediterranean garden-style terrace, the Hermitage recalls the splendour of belle époque Monaco – gaze in awe at the glass-domed atrium. A monument in its own right, it has been one of Europe's smartest hotels since it opened in the early 1900s.

Hôtel Nord-Pinus, Arles

MAP B4 ▪ 14 pl du Forum ▪ 04 65 88 40 40 ▪ Closed mid-Nov–mid-Mar ▪ www.nord-pinus. com ▪ €€

This historic hotel is the best address in Arles. The lounge and foyer have traditional Provençal decor.

Hôtel de Paris, Monte Carlo

MAP H4 ▪ Pl du Casino ▪ 00 377 98 06 30 00 ▪ www.montecarlosbm. com ▪ €€€

Rivalling the Hermitage for belle époque splendour, the Hôtel de Paris has a famous café-terrace on the ground floor *(see p110)* and is very close to the casino *(see p103)*. Queen Victoria stayed here, as have a host of other crowned heads and celebrities.

Hôtel du Cap-Eden-Roc, Antibes

MAP G4 ▪ Bd Kennedy ▪ 04 93 61 39 01 ▪ www. oetkercollection.com ▪ €€€

As ostentatious as the Negresco in its way, the Eden Roc is another landmark of the Riviera and has been since its founding in 1870. It offers exclusivity and film-star chic in tropical gardens and is, in a word, idyllic.

Hôtel Royal Riviera, St-Jean-Cap-Ferrat

MAP H4 ▪ 3 av Jean Monnet ▪ 04 93 76 31 00 ▪ www.royal-riviera.com ▪ €€€

This luxurious 1904 hotel is situated on its private beach on the Cap Ferrat peninsula. The rooms are distributed between the main building and the Orangerie. All of them are spacious with modern amenities, and many have sea views. The superb restaurant has a terrace and there's a heated pool.

La Réserve, Beaulieu

MAP H4 ▪ 5 bd du Maréchal Leclerc ▪ 04 93 01 00 01 ▪ www.reserve beaulieu.com ▪ €€€€

Opened in the late 19th century, this pink palace in its semi-tropical grounds is a grand place to stay. It still retains the glory of its 1920s heyday and exudes an air of quietly indulgent luxury.

Le Negresco, Nice

MAP P5 ▪ 37 prom des Anglais ▪ 04 93 16 64 00 ▪ www.hotel-negresco-nice.com ▪ €€€

The flagship of the whole Riviera, the Negresco is the grandest of grand hotels, from its splendid belle époque façade to its immaculate rooms and attentive service. One of the world's most opulent hotels.

Château Hotels

Château de Trigance, Trigance

MAP F3 ▪ 1400 rte de Breis ▪ 04 94 76 91 18 ▪ Closed Nov–Mar ▪ www. chateau-de-trigance.fr ▪ No air conditioning ▪ €

With just eight rooms, this small château, built in the 10th century and painstakingly restored by its owners over the last 30 years, is now a great three-star hotel. All the rooms have four-poster beds and medieval-style decor, and the restaurant is excellent.

Château de la Pioline, Aix-en-Provence

MAP C4 ▪ 260 rue Guillaume du Vair Pole ▪ 04 42 52 27 27 ▪ www.chateaude lapioline.com ▪ €€

This elegant 16th-century château is just 3 km (2 miles) from Aix. It combines historical detail with modern amenities. Some smaller rooms are in a garden outbuilding.

Château des Alpilles, St-Rémy

MAP B3 ▪ 1392 rte de Rougadou ▪ 04 90 92 03 33 ▪ www.chateau-desalpilles.com ▪ €€

The château was built in the 19th century for a prominent Arles family. The cuisine is rated highly and the rooms in the castle, former chapel and converted farmhouses are beautifully decorated.

Château de Valmer, La Croix Valmer

MAP F5 ▪ 81 bd de Gigaro ▪ 04 94 55 15 15 ▪ Closed Oct–Apr ▪ www. chateauvalmer.com ▪ No air conditioning ▪ €€

Surrounded by a 5-ha (12-acre) park with palm trees and a vine-yard, this hotel even has its own private beach.

Hôtel du Petit Palais, Nice

MAP P4 ▪ 17 av Emile Bieckert ▪ 04 93 62 19 11 ▪ www.petitpalaisnice. com ▪ €€

Set in an extensive garden, this former palace offers a quiet and scenic retreat on the hill of Cimiez. A relaxed hotel, it is renowned for its magnificent views of the city and sea.

Airelles Château de la Messardière, St-Tropez

MAP F5 ▪ 2 Rte de Tahiti ▪ 04 94 56 76 00 ▪ www. airelles.com ▪ €€€

Set on the outskirts of St-Tropez, this newly revamped seaside palace has a private beach, a luxury spa and a swimming pool. It is undoubtedly among the nicest places to stay on this fashionable part of the coast.

Château de la Chèvre d'Or, Èze

MAP H4 ▪ Rue du Barri ▪ 04 92 10 66 66 ▪ Closed Dec–Feb ▪ www.chevre dor.fr ▪ €€€

The stunning Chèvre d'Or perches high above the sea, looking out over clifftop battlements in this beautifully preserved castle-village. Rooms have a panoramic view and each one is decorated with antiques. It has three restaurants (see p110) and a pool and a spa in a pretty setting.

Château Eza, Èze

MAP H4 ▪ Rue de la Pise ▪ 04 93 41 12 24 ▪ www. chateaueza.com ▪ €€€

A wonderful collection of medieval buildings now converted into a hotel. Individually and luxuriously decorated, the 14 rooms and suites each have a marble bathroom.

Château St-Martin, Vence

MAP G4 ▪ 2490 av des Templiers ▪ 04 93 58 02 02 ▪ www.oetker collection.com ▪ €€€

This palatial hotel is set in manicured grounds on a hilltop site with views of the medieval village and the countryside. It is one of the most impressive places to stay in Provence. It offers superb service and great food.

Health and Beauty Spas

Hôtel Jules César, Arles

MAP B4 ▪ 9 bd des Lices ▪ 04 90 52 52 52 ▪ www. hotel-julescesar.fr ▪ €

In 2014, Christian Lacroix set about transforming this 17th-century former Carmelite convent in Arles city centre into a chic, boutique hotel. It has a Cinq Mondes spa and a heated pool in the garden cloister.

Le Mas de la Crémaillère, Gréoux-les-Bains

MAP D3 ▪ Rte de Riez ▪ 04 92 70 40 04 ▪ Closed mid-Dec–Mar ▪ www. mascremailleregreoux. com ▪ €

A range of spa packages at the sulphur-rich thermal springs of Gréoux-les-Bains is available to guests in this farmhouse-hotel. It has a swimming pool, golf practice range and a restaurant noted for its Provençal menu.

Hôtel le Couvent des Minimes, Mane

MAP D3 ▪ Chemin des Jeux de Mai ▪ 04 92 74 77 77 ▪ www.couvent desminimes-hotelspa. com ▪ €€

This beautiful former convent boasts the first L'Occitane hotel spa, along with a pool, an aromatic garden, two restaurants and a bar. The hotel is closed for renovation and will reopen in 2023.

La Maison de la Sorgue, L'Isle-sur-la-Sorgue

MAP C3 ▪ 6 rue Rose Goudarde ▪ 06 87 32 58 68 ▪ www.lamaison surlasorgue.com ▪ €€

Furnishings from around the world and cutting-edge mod cons fill rooms and suites in this stunning 17th-century town house, with a secret garden and pool by the river.

Le Domaine de la Rose, Orgon

MAP C3 ▪ Rte d'Eygalières ▪ 04 90 73 08 91 ▪ www. mas-rose.com ▪ €€

Set in a vast park of pines, lavender and olive groves, these 17th-century stone bergeries (farm buildings) have been transformed into the chic rooms of an elegant hotel.

Les Rosées, Mougins

MAP G4 ▪ 238 Chemin de Font Neuve ▪ 04 92 92 29 64 ▪ www.les rosees.com ▪ €€

A haven of peace and beauty: you can choose between four differently decorated suites in a medieval farmhouse, or a romantic, shabby-chic gypsy caravan at the bottom of the garden.

Hôtel Sezz, St-Tropez

MAP F5 ▪ 151 rte des Salins ▪ 04 94 55 31 55 ▪ www.saint-tropez. hotelsezz.com ▪ €€€

Rooms at this chic and minimalist hotel, just outside St-Tropez, all come with private garden terraces and outdoor showers. There's a spa and an idyllic palm-lined pool, plus a free shuttle service into town.

Le Mas de Pierre, St-Paul-de-Vence

MAP G4 ▪ 2320 rte des Serres ▪ 04 93 59 00 10 ▪ www.lemasdepierre. com ▪ €€€

Located in the beautiful countryside outside of St-Paul-de-Vence, this luxurious four-star hotel has been designed to help its guests relax. Facilities include a rose garden with stunning views, a hammam and a pool.

Tiara Yaktsa Côte d'Azur, Théoule-sur-Mer

MAP G4 ▪ 6 bd de l'Esquillon ▪ 04 92 28 60 30 ▪ yaktsa.tiara-hotels. com ▪ €€€€

This relaxing hideaway is perched amid verdant tropical gardens on the wild Esterel coast. It has bars, restaurants, an infinity pool, a private beach and spa access.

Super Hideaways

Hôtel des Deux Rocs, Seillans

MAP F4 ▪ Pl Font d'Amont ▪ 04 94 76 87 32 ▪ www.hoteldeuxrocs. com ▪ No air conditioning ▪ €

Located in a perfectly preserved medieval hill village, this is charming in an old-fashioned way. It has a delightful terrace on a tiny cobbled square, and a restaurant serving great Provençal cooking.

Hôtel Villa la Roseraie, Vence

MAP G4 ▪ 128 av Henri Giraud, rte de Course-goules ▪ 04 93 58 02 20 ▪ www.villaroseraie. com ▪ €

This friendly small hotel has a pool and gardens,

and the rooms are charming. It's ideal for a romantic weekend away at an affordable price.

Moulin de la Camandoule, Fayence

MAP F4 ▪ 159 chemin de Notre-Dame ▪ 04 94 76 00 84 ▪ www.camando ule.com ▪ No air conditioning ▪ €

A swimming pool shaded beneath trees, excellent food and a delightful location hidden away among vines and pines make this converted olive mill one of the most peaceful and pleasant places to stay.

Grande Bastide, St-Paul-de-Vence

MAP G4 ▪ Rte de la Colle ▪ 04 93 32 50 30 ▪ www. la-grande-bastide.com ▪ €€

This converted country house is just outside St-Paul-de-Vence (though it's too far to walk, except for the most energetic). It is calm, friendly and peaceful, with a pool under palm trees and an immaculately kept garden. The rooms and suites are furnished and decorated in Provençal-style fabrics, and there are beautiful views.

La Pérouse, Nice

MAP P5 ▪ 11 quai Rauba Capeu ▪ 04 93 62 34 63 ▪ www.hotel-la-perouse. com ▪ €€

This hidden luxury retreat has one of the best views of Nice's lovely promenade. Choose a sea-view room with its own terrace. There's a pretty dining courtyard and a rooftop hot tub as well.

Le Cagnard, Cagnes-sur-Mer

MAP G4 ▪ 54 rue Sous-Barri ▪ 04 93 20 73 22 ▪ www.lecagnard.fr ▪ €€

Only a few minutes' drive from the hurly-burly of the Riviera, Le Cagnard is a luxury inn, with lovely rooms in a medieval building, sweeping views and a fine restaurant. All this, and it's located in a pretty village smothered in purple bougainvillea.

Le Mas d'Aigret, Les-Baux-de-Provence

MAP B4 ▪ D27A, Chemin de Baubesse ▪ 04 90 54 20 00 ▪ www.masdaigret. com ▪ €€

A charming character hotel with two troglodytic rooms, partly carved from limestone. It has an excellent restaurant and terrace, and is well-placed to explore the village as well as castle.

La Ponche, St-Tropez

MAP F5 ▪ 5 rue des Remparts ▪ 04 94 97 02 53 ▪ Closed Nov–mid-Mar ▪ www.laponche.com ▪ €€€

Stylish, individual and hidden in a tiny square with a view of the fishing port, it is the perfect place to escape the bustle of the town in summer.

La Villa Mauresque, St Raphaël

MAP F5 ▪ 1792 rte de la Corniche, Boulouris ▪ 04 94 83 02 42 ▪ www.villa-mauresque.com ▪ €€€€

On a secret cove near St-Raphaël, this Moorish-style villa was built for a pasha in 1860. In 2013 it was restored as a superb luxury hotel, immersed in lush, exotic gardens.

Value-for-Money Hotels

Hôtel 96, Marseille
MAP C5 ▪ 96 av de la Soude ▪ 04 91 71 90 22 ▪ www.hotel96.com ▪ €
A small, but attractive family hotel located among pleasant gardens, Hôtel 96 offers a hearty breakfast and facilities such as a swimming pool and sauna. The rooms have contemporary decor and the hotel itself is a short bicycle ride away from the beaches.

Hôtel Ambassador, Monaco
MAP H4 ▪ 10 av Prince-Pierre ▪ 00 377 97 97 96 96 ▪ www.ambassador monaco.com ▪ €
This modern hotel could not be better located, right in the heart of Monaco, at the foot of the Prince's Palace. All the rooms are well equipped, with a TV, hairdryer and internet access, and the on-site restaurant serves basic Italian cuisine, including good, inexpensive pizzas.

Hôtel Avaton, Cannes
MAP G4 ▪ 6 rue Emile-Négrin ▪ 04 93 39 53 90 ▪ www.avatonhotel. com ▪ €
Tucked away in a narrow street not far from the yacht harbour, this small hotel, offering a breath-taking view of the port, is quite possibly the best bargain in Cannes. The service is friendly, and the rooms here are simple, but clean and brightly lit (some have balconies with a sea view), with phone, TV and internet connection.

Hôtel le Calendal, Arles
MAP B4 ▪ 5 rue Porte de Laure ▪ 04 90 96 11 89 ▪ www.lecalendal.com ▪ €
A colourful place to stay in a vibrant city, the Calendal is brightly decorated and has a pretty, well-shaded garden café and a vaulted spa. Some of the more expensive rooms have terraces and are air conditioned, making this three-star hotel a great-value place to stay in the otherwise expensive Arles.

Le Windsor, Nice
MAP H4 ▪ 11 rue Dalpozzo ▪ 04 93 88 59 35 ▪ www.hotelwindsor nice.com ▪ €
Artist-decorated rooms with hand-painted murals, a swimming pool surrounded by palm trees and alfresco meals come at an affordable price in this hotel.

Hôtel La Jabotte, Cap d'Antibes
MAP G4 ▪ 13 av Max-Maurey ▪ 04 93 61 45 89 ▪ www.jabotte.com ▪ No air conditioning ▪ €€
With its clean, bright rooms and chalets and good location, La Jabotte is one of the better bargains in upmarket Antibes. It also has its own car park – quite a rarity in Cap d'Antibes.

Hôtel Splendid, Cannes
MAP G4 ▪ 4 rue Félix Faure ▪ 04 97 06 22 22 ▪ www.splendid-hotel-cannes.com ▪ €€
Value for money doesn't always mean cheap, but the Splendid, centrally located close to the yacht harbour, is an impressive hotel and is a bargain by Cannes standards.

Le Benvengudo, Les-Baux-de-Provence
MAP B4 ▪ Vallon de l'Arcoule ▪ 04 90 54 32 54 ▪ www.benvengudo. com ▪ €€
This charming hotel proves that value is not all about price: it has comfortable, beautifully decorated rooms (some with their own large terrace), a pool, garden, restaurant and tennis court, and all in lovely surroundings.

Gîtes and Chambres d'Hôtes

Le Gîte de Chasteuil, Castellane
MAP F3 ▪ Hameau de Chasteuil ▪ 06 73 56 31 43 ▪ www.gitede chasteuil.com ▪ No air conditioning ▪ €
This delightful bed-and-breakfast is high on a hillside in a tiny hamlet close to the east end of the Canyon du Verdon, with mountain views. For walkers, the GR4 long-distance footpath passes right through the village. Each bedroom has its own bathroom, and one has a kitchenette.

Le Hameau de Pichovet, Vachères
MAP D3 ▪ Campagne Pichovet ▪ 04 92 73 33 48 ▪ www.hameau-de-pichovet.com ▪ No air conditioning ▪ €
Situated close to the lavender fields of the Luberon National Park, this stone house offers four guest rooms and two apartments. The pool is heated from mid-May to mid-October, and the restaurant provides

authentic dishes at a family-style dining table or on the terrace.

Le Mas de la Beaume, Gordes

MAP C3 ▪ 04 90 72 02 96 ▪ www.labeaume.com ▪ No air conditioning ▪ €

Throw open the windows and look out onto the Alpilles mountains or the château of Gordes from this delightful old farmhouse. The three rooms and two suites are individually decorated and furnished with quirky antiques and fine linens. The swimming pool is hidden in an olive grove, and breakfast comes with home-made jams.

L'Hemmitage, Salernes

MAP E4 ▪ 683 chemin la Pouade ▪ 06 89 43 75 10 ▪ www.hemmitage. com ▪ No credit cards ▪ €

Painted a striking pink, this farmhouse set in vineyards and orchards has eight holiday homes named after famous painters. Each has its own kitchenette and terrace. During high season, a minimum booking period of one week is mandatory.

Maison du Frêne, Vence

MAP G4 ▪ 1 place du Frêne ▪ 06 88 90 49 69 ▪ www.lamaisondufrene. com ▪ €

A delightful melange of Baroque, this arty 18th-century town house is located in the centre of Vence, opposite, appropri-ately enough, the Museum of Modern Art. There are four spacious suites and a shared lounge, and rates include free Wi-Fi and a generous French breakfast.

La Prévôté, L'Isle-sur-la-Sorgue

MAP C3 ▪ 4 rue Jean-Jacques Rousseau ▪ 04 90 38 57 29 ▪ www. la-prevote.fr ▪ No air conditioning ▪ €€

"A well-kept secret among friends" is the motto of this B&B, set in a former monastery. Rooms are spacious and stylish, and the gourmet restaurant uses only fresh, local produce.

Les Roullets, Oppède

MAP C3 ▪ 305a chemin de Fontdrèche ▪ 04 90 71 21 88 ▪ www.lesroullets. com ▪ €€

High on the hill of a Roman oppidum, this luxurious six-room B&B occupies a stone-built farmhouse. It has a heated pool and beautiful grounds with a 700-year-old tree.

Camping

Camping Abri de Camargue, Le-Grau-du-Roi

MAP A4 ▪ 320 rte du Phare de l'Espiguette ▪ 04 66 51 54 83 ▪ Closed Oct–Mar ▪ www. abridecamargue.fr ▪ €

This clean, medium-sized campsite is near a sandy beach. It has indoor and outdoor pools, a play area, cinema, bar, shop and restaurant, and *boules* and tennis courts nearby.

Camping du Domaine, Bormes-les-Mimosas

MAP E5 ▪ 2581 rte de Bénat ▪ 04 94 71 03 12 ▪ Closed Nov–Mar ▪ www.campdu domaine.com ▪ €

A stone's throw from the sea, this leafy five-star family-oriented campsite also rents out bungalows

and mobile homes. It has many sports facilities and a free children's mini-club.

Camping Eden, Biot

MAP G4 ▪ 63 chemin du Val de Pôme ▪ 04 93 65 63 70 ▪ Closed Nov–Mar ▪ www.camping-eden.fr ▪ €

At the foot of the village of Biot, this campsite has a swimming pool and a terrace restaurant, plus an on-site grocery store that sells fresh baguettes and croissants every morning. There's a beach nearby; Antibes is also next door.

Camping la Pinède, Grimaud

MAP F5 ▪ 1968 rte de Ste-Maxime ▪ 04 94 56 04 36 ▪ Closed Nov–Mar ▪ www.capfun.com ▪ €

A cheap and cheerful alternative to St-Tropez's hotels – with facilities that include a mini-golf course, a children's play area, a restaurant and a snack bar.

Camping le Pesquier, Castellane

MAP F3 ▪ RN 85, rte de Digne-les-Bains ▪ 04 92 83 66 81 ▪ Closed Oct–Mar ▪ www.camping-le-pesquier.com ▪ €

This two-star site has a small pool, and tents are pitched under shady trees.

Huttopia Fontvieille

MAP B4 ▪ Rue Michelet ▪ 04 90 54 78 69 ▪ Closed mid-Oct–Mar ▪ www. europe.huttopia.com ▪ €

Located in the heart of the Alpilles Regional Park, this modern site in a pine forest has a heated outdoor pool and organizes children's activities in summer.

General Index

Acknowledgments

Authors

Robin Gauldie is a travel journalist who has visited Provence regularly since 1972. After several years working for the *Travel Trade Gazette*, Robin is now a freelance journalist and author of more than a dozen guidebooks to destinations ranging from Greece to Goa.

Lancashire-born Anthony Peregrine lives in the Languedoc region of southern France, and works as an author and journalist specializing in food, wine and travel. His work has appeared in the *Daily Telegraph*, *Daily Mail* and BBC Radio 4.

Additional contributors
Dana Facaros and Tristan Rutherford

Publishing Director Georgina Dee

Publisher Vivien Antwi

Design Director Phil Ormerod

Editorial Michelle Crane, Rachel Fox, Fay Franklin, Sally Schafer, Beverly Smart, Hollie Teague, Rachel Thompson, Sophie Wright

Cover Design Bess Daly, Maxine Pedliham

Design Tessa Bindloss, Richard Czapnik, Bharti Karakoti

Picture Research Susie Peachey, Ellen Root, Lucy Sienkowska, Oran Tarjan

Cartography James Macdonald

Senior Production Editor Jason Little

Production Nancy-Jane Maun

Factchecker Lyn Parry

Proofreader Susanne Hillen

Indexer Helen Peters

Illustrator Chris Orr & Associates

First edition created by Sargasso Media Ltd, London

Revisions Avanika, Subhashree Bharati, Dipika Dasgupta, Robert Harneis, Sumita Khatwani, Shikha Kulkarni, Vagisha Pushp, Rada Radojicic, M. Astella Saw, Ankita Sharma, Azeem Siddiqui, Priyanka Thakur, Stuti Tiwari, Vinita Venugopal, Tanveer Zaidi

Commissioned Photography Demetrio Carrasco, Rough Guides/Michelle Grant, Alan Williams

24-5; Photogolfer 102tl; Photoprofi30 68tr; Beatrice Preve 124cla; Luca Quadrio 28-9, 38cl; Radomír Režný 4clb; Santiago Rodríguez Fontoba 16br; Guy Rouget 10cl, 89cl, 90b; Rudiuk 116br; Alexander Sandvoss 69tl; Juergen Schonnop 15crb; Richard Semik 29crb, 80ca; Stevanzz 39b; Tramontana 50t; Travelpeter 4cl; Valentina1605 84b; Willyvend 65tr; Maren Winter 81tl; Oleg Znamenskiy 49tl; Znm 30-1c; Zorro12 76tl.

La Ferme aux Crocodiles: 63br.

Getty Images: DeAgostini/S. Vannini 2tr, 34-5; Hans Georg Eiben 11crb, 18-9; AFP / Francois Guillot 37br; Peter Zelei Images 2tl, 8-9; M G Therin Weise 25crb.

Hotel du-Cap-Eden-Roc: 61br.

Hôtel Restaurant Les Deux Frères: 111cr.

iStockphoto.com: bwzenith 33tl, Siempreverde22 11br, StevanZZ 1.

L'Esprit de la Violette: Martial Thiebaut 85cl.

Le Louis XV - Alain Ducasse à l'Hôtel de Paris: Pierre Monetta 62t.

Mary Evans Picture Library: BeBa/Iberfoto 36br.

Monte-Carlo S.B.M. Hotels and Casinos: 109cl; JJL Heritier 103tl.

Nice Tourism: J. Kelagopian 69cl.

Palais des Festivals et des Congrès de Cannes: Semec-Fabre 108clb; Semec-Perreard 106b.

Rex by Shutterstock: Chris Hellier 71tr; PhotoAlto 46tl; Isa Harsin 96tl; Universal History Archive/ Universal Images Group 41bl; WestEnd6 75t.

Robert Harding Picture Library: Christophe Boisvieux 105bl; Martin Child 87tl; Werner Dieterich 82cl; Godong 19tc; Amanda Hall 20-1; Peter Schickert 127cl; Valery Trillaud 113br; Ken Welsh 115cl.

Office de Tourisme de Saint-Raphaël: G. Derivière 88br.

Sens et Saveurs: 123clb.

The Art Archive: Archaeological Museum Vaison-la-Romaine /Gianni Dagli Orti 28bc.

Toinou: 79tr.

Var Tourisme: JH Walzl 88tl.

Vaucluse Tourisme: 126cl, 130cla, Alain Hocquel 28cl.

Photo Villa Arson: Architecte Michel Marot & Ass (1970) 66tl.

Cover

Front and spine: **iStockphoto.com:** StevanZZ.

Back: **AWL Images:** Jon Arnold cla; **iStockphoto. com:** StevanZZ b; **Dreamstime.com:** Claudio Giovanni Colombo crb, Margouillat tl, Xantana tr .

Pull Out Map Cover

iStockphoto.com: StevanZZ

All other images © Dorling Kindersley
For further information see: www.dkimages.com

Penguin Random House

Printed and bound in China

First edition 2002

Published in Great Britain by Dorling Kindersley Limited DK, One Embassy Gardens, 8 Viaduct Gardens, London SW11 7BW

The authorised representative in the EEA is Dorling Kindersley Verlag GmbH. Arnulfstr. 124, 80636 Munich, Germany

Published in the United States by DK Publishing, 1450 Broadway, Suite 801, New York, NY 10018

Copyright © 2002, 2022 Dorling Kindersley Limited

A Penguin Random House Company

22 23 24 10 9 8 7 6 5 4 3 2 1

Reprinted with revisions 2003, 2004, 2006, 2008, 2010, 2012, 2014, 2017, 2019, 2022

A CIP catalogue record is available from the British Library.

A catalogue record for this book is available from the Library of Congress.

ISSN 1479-344X

ISBN 978-0-2414-7219-4

As a guide to abbreviations in visitor information blocks: **Adm** = admission charge; **D** = dinner; **L** = lunch.

MIX
Paper from responsible sources
FSC www.fsc.org FSC™ C018179

This book was made with Forest Stewardship Council ™ certified paper – one small step in DK's commitment to a sustainable future. For more information go to www.dk.com/our-green-pledge

Phrase Book

In an Emergency

Help!	Au secours!	oh sekoor
Stop!	Arrêtez!	aret-ay
Call…	Appelez…	apuh-lay
…a doctor!	…un médecin!	uñ medsañ
…an ambulance!	…une ambulance!	oon oñboo-loñs
…the police!	…la police!	lah poh-lees
…the fire brigade!	…les pompiers!	leh poñ-peeyay

Communication Essentials

Yes/No	Oui/Non	wee/noñ
Please	S'il vous plaît	seel voo play
Thank you	Merci	mer-see
Excuse me	Excusez-moi	exkoo-zay mwah
Hello	Bonjour	boñzhoor
Goodbye	Au revoir	oh ruh-vwar
Good night	Bonsoir	boñ-swar
What?	Quel, quelle?	kel, kel
When?	Quand?	koñ
Why?	Pourquoi?	poor-kwah
Where?	Où?	oo

Useful Phrases

How are you?	Comment allez-vous?	kom-moñ talay voo
Very well, Pleased to meet you.	Très bien, Enchanté de faire votre connaissance.	treh byañ oñshoñ-tuy duh fehr votr kon-ay-sans
Where is/are…?	Où est/sont…?	oo ay/soñ
Which way to..?	Quelle est la direction pour..?	kel ay lah deer-ek-syoñ poor
Do you speak English?	Parlez-vous anglais?	pur-lay voo oñg-lay
I don't understand.	Je ne comprends pas.	zhuh nuh kom-proñ pah
I'm sorry.	Excusez-moi.	exkoo-zay mwah

Useful Words

big	grand	groñ
small	petit	puh-tee
hot	chaud	show
cold	froid	frwah
good	bon	boñ
bad	mauvais	moh-veh
open	ouvert	oo-ver
closed	fermé	fer-meh
left	gauche	gohsh
right	droit	drwah
entrance	l'entrée	l'on-tray
exit	la sortie	sor-tee
toilet	les toilettes	twah-let

Shopping

How much is it?	Ça fait combien?	sa fay kom-byañ
What time…	A quelle heure…	ah kel urr
…do you open?	…êtes-vous ouvert?	et-voo oo-ver
…do you close?	…êtes-vous fermé?	et-voo fer-may
Do you have?	Est-ce que vous avez?	es-kuh voo zavay
I would like …	Je voudrais…	zhuh voo-dray
Do you take credit cards?	Est-ce que vous acceptez les cartes de crédit?	es-kuh voo zaksept-ay leh kart duh krehdee
This one.	Celui-ci.	suhl-wee-see
That one.	Celui-là.	suhl-wee-lah
expensive	cher	shehr
cheap	pas cher, bon marché,	pah shehr, boñ mar-shay
size, clothes	la taille	tye
size, shoes	la pointure	pwañ-tur

Types of Shop

antique shop	le magasin d'antiquités	maga-zañ d'oñteekee-tay
bakery	la boulangerie	booloñ-zhuree
bank	la banque	boñk
bookshop	la librairie	lee-brehree
cake shop	la pâtisserie	patee-sree
cheese shop	la fromagerie	fromazh-ree
chemist	la pharmacie	farmah-see
department store	le grand magasin	groñ maga-zañ
delicatessen	la charcuterie	sharkoot-ree
gift shop	le magasin de cadeaux	maga-zañ duh kadoh
greengrocer	le marchand de légumes	mar-shoñ duh lay-goom
grocery	l'alimentation	alee-moñtasyoñ
market	le marché	marsh-ay
newsagent	le magasin de journaux	maga-zañ duh zhoor-no
post office	la poste, le bureau de poste, le PTT	pohst, hooroh duh pohst, peh-teh-teh
supermarket	le supermarché	soo pehr-marshay
tobacconist	le tabac	tabah
travel agent	l'agence de voyages	l'azhoñs duh vwayazh

Sightseeing

art gallery	la galerie d'art	galer-ree dart
bus station	la gare routière	gahr roo-tee-yehr
cathedral	la cathédrale	katay-dral
church	l'église	l'aygleez
garden	le jardin	zhar-dañ
library	la bibliothèque	beebleeo-tek
museum	le musée	moo-zay
railway station	la gare (SNCF)	gahr (es-en-say-ef)
tourist office	l'office du tourisme	ohfees doo tooreesm
town hall	l'hôtel de ville	l'ohtel duh veel

Staying in a Hotel

Do you have a vacant room?	Est-ce que vous avez une chambre?	es-kuh voo-zavay oon shambr
I have a reservation.	J'ai fait une réservation.	zhay fay oun rayzehrva-syoñ
single room	la chambre à une personne	shambr ah oon pehr-son
twin room	la chambre à deux lits	shambr ah duh lee
room with a bath, shower	la chambre avec salle de bains, une douche	shambr avek sal duh bañ, oon doosh

double room, with a double bed	la chambre à deux personnes avec un grand lit	shambr ah duh pehr-son avek un gronñ lee

Eating Out

Have you got a table?	Avez-vous une table libre?	avay-voo oon tahbl duh leebr
I want to reserve a table.	Je voudrais réserver une table.	zhuh voo-dray rayzehr-vay oon tahbl
The bill, please.	L'addition, s'il vous plaît.	l'adee-syoñ seel voo play
Waitress/ waiter	Madame, Mademoiselle/ Monsieur	mah-dam, mah-demwahzel/ muh-syuh
menu	le menu, la carte	men-oo, kart
fixed-price menu	le menu à prix fixe	men-oo ah pree feeks
cover charge	le couvert	koo-vehr
wine list	la carte des vins	kart-deh vañ
glass	le verre	vehr
bottle	la bouteille	boo-tay
knife	le couteau	koo-toh
fork	la fourchette	for-shet
spoon	la cuillère	kwee-yehr
breakfast	le petit déjeuner	puh-tee deh-zhuh-nay
lunch	le déjeuner	deh-zhuh-nay
dinner	le dîner	dee-nay
main course	le plat principal	plah prañsee-pal
starter, first course	l'entrée, le hors d'oeuvre	l'oñ-tray, or-duhvr
dish of the day	le plat du jour	plah doo zhoor
wine bar	le bar à vin	bar ah vañ
café	le café	ka-fay

Menu Decoder

baked	cuit au four	kweet oh foor
beef	le boeuf	buhf
beer	la bière	bee-yehr
boiled	bouilli	boo-yee
bread	le pain	pan
butter	le beurre	burr
cake	le gâteau	gah-toh
cheese	le fromage	from-azh
chicken	le poulet	poo-lay
chips	les frites	freet
chocolate	le chocolat	shoko-lah
coffee	le café	kah-fay
dessert	le dessert	deh-ser
duck	le canard	kanar
egg	l'oeuf	l'uf
fish	le poisson	pwah-ssoñ
fresh fruit	le fruit frais	frwee freh
garlic	l'ail	l'eye
grilled	grillé	gree-yay
ham	le jambon	zhoñ-boñ
ice, ice cream	la glace	glas
lamb	l'agneau	l'anyoh
lemon	le citron	see-troñ
fresh lemon juice	le citron pressé	see-troñ presseh
meat	la viande	vee-yand
milk	le lait	leh
mineral water	l'eau minérale	l'oh meeney-ral
oil	l'huile	l'weel

onions	les oignons	leh zonyoñ
orange juice	l'orange pressée	l'oroñzh presseh
pepper	le poivre	pwavr
pork	le porc	por
potatoes	les pommes de terre	pom duh tehr
rice	le riz	ree
roast	rôti	row-tee
salt	le sel	sel
sausage	la saucisse	sohsees
seafood	les fruits de mer	frwee duh mer
snails	les escargots	leh zes-kar-goh
soup	la soupe, le potage	soop, poh-tazh
steak	le bifteck, le steak	beef-tek, stek
sugar	le sucre	sookr
tea	le thé	tay
vegetables	les légumes	lay-goom
vinegar	le vinaigre	veenaygr
water	l'eau	l'oh
red wine	le vin rouge	vañ roozh
white wine	le vin blanc	vañ bloñ

Numbers

0	zéro	zeh-roh
1	un, une	uñ, oon
2	deux	duh
3	trois	trwah
4	quatre	katr
5	cinq	sañk
6	six	sees
7	sept	set
8	huit	weet
9	neuf	nerf
10	dix	dees
11	onze	oñz
12	douze	dooz
13	treize	trehz
14	quatorze	katorz
15	quinze	kañz
16	seize	sehz
17	dix-sept	dees-set
18	dix-huit	dees-weet
19	dix-neuf	dees-nerf
20	vingt	vañ
30	trente	tront
40	quarante	karoñt
50	cinquante	sañkoñt
60	soixante	swasoñt
70	soixante-dix	swasoñt-dees
80	quatre-vingts	katr-vañ
90	quatre-vingt-dix	katr-vañ-dees
100	cent	soñ
1,000	mille	meel

Time

one minute	une minute	oon mee-noot
one hour	une heure	oon urr
half an hour	une demi-heure	urr duh-me urr
one day	un jour	urr zhorr
Monday	lundi	luñ-dee
Tuesday	mardi	mar-dee
Wednesday	mercredi	mehrkruh-dee
Thursday	jeudi	zhuh-dee
Friday	vendredi	voñdruh-dee
Saturday	samedi	sam-dee
Sunday	dimanche	dee-moñsh